At David C Cook, we equip the local church around the corner and around the globe to make disciples. Come see how we are working together—go to **www.davidccook.org**. Thank you!

transforming lives together

What people are saying about …

Hidden Potential

"We all have past experiences and personal struggles that make us feel disqualified from serving God. Fears and faults taunt us by saying, 'There's no way God will ever use you.' Thankfully, Wendy's wise, biblically sound teaching will help you think differently and step into your calling more confidently. Not only is Wendy a dear friend but also a reassuring voice of Truth."

Lysa TerKeurst, #1 *New York Times* bestselling author and president of Proverbs 31 Ministries

"Wendy Pope has dug deep, to our good and God's glory. *Hidden Potential* is a must read and a reread for all who are willing to own their ugly before the God who can love us whole, fit us for His purposes, and delight us in the process."

Shellie Rushing Tomlinson, author of *Finding Deep and Wide*

"Are you struggling to believe that God can use you to do mighty things for Him? There's no limit to what He can do through you. *Hidden Potential* is a prescription for those whose faith is 'fractured.'

God wants to use you (mightily) for His glory! I loved the book! It's powerful and applicable to all."

Sharon Glasgow, author and speaker
with Proverbs 31 Ministries

"Illustrated through the biblical account of the life of Moses, and present-day believers like you and me, Wendy shows you how to be faithful even when you're afraid, useful when you've failed, and valuable even though you feel damaged. This book is not empty encouragement; it will show you how to read the Bible and apply it to your life, to restore hope and heal the wounds that keep you from experiencing the abundant life."

Timothy W. Peterson, publisher of Salem Books

"With the wisdom of a mentor and the honesty of a friend, Wendy Pope reminds us that our potential isn't tied to our perfection, and our purpose isn't hindered by our flaws. Savor the stunning truth on these pages, friends, and start dreaming bigger! God is ready and willing to use us for His glory just as we are."

Alicia Bruxvoort, member of the
Proverbs 31 Ministries writing team

What readers are saying about …

Hidden Potential

"*Hidden Potential* will convict you, shake you up, and may even make you a little mad. But it will also raise the hairs on the back of your neck as you realize that the God of the universe sees so much more in you than you ever could!"

"I needed this right now in this season of my life. I walked away from reading this 100 percent ready and willing to surrender those grey areas of my life to God."

"I felt like [the author] knew me—knew I have a place I like to go to hide. I also enjoyed her encouragement not to stay there but to return and face my failure."

"'Do you believe God can for others, but not for you?' I'd never put it that way, but I've thought it to myself so many times. [This book] started to open my heart to the realization that I'm not the only person who feels unworthy."

"Wendy Pope delivered hard truth in a loving way. Who wants to admit that they deal with failures, faults, fears, and frailties? Nobody, typically. We sweep it under the rug and hope nobody notices. She takes the reader by the hand and says, this may not be easy to confront, but it's necessary in order to live up to your godly potential."

"I loved the way she weaved the story of Moses into the entire book. It was masterful the way she shared his story in a fresh, new way."

Hidden Potential

Hidden Potential

Revealing What God Can
Do through You

Wendy Pope

DAVID **C** COOK

transforming lives together

HIDDEN POTENTIAL
Published by David C Cook
4050 Lee Vance Drive
Colorado Springs, CO 80918 U.S.A.

Integrity Music Limited, a Division of David C Cook
Brighton, East Sussex BN1 2RE, England

The graphic circle C logo is a registered trademark of David C Cook.

The website addresses recommended throughout this book are offered as a
resource to you. These websites are not intended in any way to be or imply an
endorsement on the part of David C Cook, nor do we vouch for their content.

Bible credits are listed at the back of the book.

Library of Congress Control Number 2019948090
ISBN 978-1-4347-1237-0
eISBN 978-0-8307-7916-1

The Team: Laura Derico, Megan Stengel, Jack Campbell, Susan Murdock
Cover Design: Jon Middel
Cover Photo: Getty Images

Printed in the United States of America
First Edition 2020

1 2 3 4 5 6 7 8 9 10

121619

Dedicated to the women of
The Move Conference 2016
Lansing, MI
"You are a worthwhile possibility."

Contents

Acknowledgments

Hidden Potential was written largely in part due to an invitation from my Midwestern sista, Keturah. Speaking at the Move Conference sparked the embers of this message. "You are a worthwhile possibility" was birthed that weekend. I love you, friend, and the Move Conference girls.

Sharon, Sheri, Meg, and Linda, I can't thank you enough for bearing your heart and soul to the audience of *Hidden Potential*. Each of you means so much to me. Your contribution to this work will facilitate healing in the lives of women around the world. I love each of you and have loved watching your potential reveal itself as you have surrendered your lives for His glory.

I have the best publishing team at David C Cook: Annette, Laura, Susan, Megan, Nick, Jon, and Jack. Thank you for teaching me so much about publishing and not holding against me what I don't know. I'm grateful to be partnering with you on another powerful message.

Thank you to Lysa TerKeurst and my Proverbs 31 Ministries family for your love, support, and training.

Blythe, I love you! You are undoubtedly the best Christian Literary Agent in the business. Anyone looking for an agent?

Daddy and Momma, I'm living the life I have because of you. Serving you during these senior years is one of God's biggest blessings to me.

I have the best people! Scott, Blaire, and Griffin—our family is the most important thing in this world to me. I pray your fears, faults, failures, and frailties never hold you back from God's great plan for your lives. You are a worthwhile possibility!

Introduction

If you could change anything about you, what would it be?

I'm sure my list would be completely different from yours, or maybe you look at me and assume I don't have a list. Oh, I have two: one from child me and one from current me. The child me wanted blond hair, and yes, because it seemed like they had more fun and were more popular. Child me wanted blue eyes to go with the blond hair. I wanted my jeans to be Gloria Vanderbilt or Jordache, and my shirts to have an alligator—not a ladybug pretending to be an alligator. Oh, and to be smart, you know, on the A/B honor roll. These things seem silly now that I'm grown, but grown women have lists too.

Current me wants to be twenty pounds lighter and have wrinkles only in clothes. I'd love to know what *she* knows about the Bible (whoever *she* is). And it would be fantabulous if my house could stay clean like *hers*. This ideal *she* is further along in ministry than I (and I started before her!). Current me still has so much work to do.

That's what we do, isn't it? We habitually compare our insides, how we feel about ourselves, to another's outside, how they look, to determine our value and sum up our potential—appearance, accomplishments, and assets. We look at other girls and think: *She has the beauty and talent of singer Whitney Houston, the success of J. K. Rowling, and the influence of Marlee Matlin. I'm sure she doesn't hear the echo of negative and condemning thoughts in the empty places of her heart. There's no way she wrestles with the weight of fears, faults, failures, and frailties—she doesn't have any!*

Out in the world we have to prove our abilities, demonstrate our intellect, and establish our authority in order to show we are useful and worthwhile. But what about in a safe, supposedly judgment-free zone, like inside the walls of the church? Do we think we have to prove ourselves there too? Do we make assumptions about someone's worth based on what they do or how they look? Without pause, yes, yes, we do. We look at *her* outside—appearance, accomplishments, and other assets—and assume *her* faith is just as strong.

She has every question completed in her Bible study. Her responses in small group are always deep and profound. Her house is immaculate, and those children, well, they never misbehave. What doesn't she do? Everything turns out right for her. There is no way she struggles with her faith. She's on the short list for sainthood. I'm sure her past is as clean as the Colorado snow on a winter day.

May I ask you to honestly answer a few questions? Not necessarily out loud, or even on paper where someone might see your answers, but just for yourself.

- Do I allow the echo of fears and faults to silence God's voice?
- Do I dwell on failures and let them determine my direction?
- Do I worry that my frailties disqualify me from doing any good work for God?

If you answered *yes* to just one of these questions, then your faith, my friend, is wounded. Fractured. Splintered. Ruptured. No longer in its original design or even what it once was before life happened to you. The original design of our faith is to be Christ-centered, Spirit-led, and Word-fed. Somehow, you, like so many of us, have gotten off track.

When we first come to learn about Jesus and His love for us, we have every intention to stay in that love. Once you know what it feels like to be loved just for who you are and just as you are, why would anyone want to move away from that? We want to learn more about the God who saved us. We may even see ourselves serving Him all our lives.

But then, often without warning, an accusing memory targets our belief that God can really wash away our sin and make us new. An old or new fear consumes our spirit and devours our courage. Our frailty shouts louder than truth, and the portfolio of our faults overwhelms our sense of purpose. Before long, the point of the splinter has pricked our heart, the assurance of our faith ruptures, and ugly thoughts fill our mind.

Fractures can be repaired—just consult any orthopedic surgeon. Bones and tissue can be reset and repaired, almost as good as new.

But what about our faith? Can it be repaired, reset, or made better than before? Or are we condemned to a powerless life full of regret?

I want to say something that may sound a little harsh, momentarily make you mad, and quite possibly give you an overwhelming desire to throw this book out a window. So, I ask you to trust me enough to read the entire statement below, pause to think through the words, and perhaps even pray.

What if God's plan isn't to "fix" the things that have fractured your faith but instead to show His power through them, making your faith stronger than ever?

[Insert pause.]

Whew. There, I said it. Are you still with me? Oh, I hope so!

God has such a good word for us, friends! Yes, us. I'm writing this book for me, as much as I am for you. I've spent much of my life trying to conquer my fears, correct my faults, get over my failures, and accept my frailties, only to discover I still have fears, faults, failures, and frailties. Can anyone relate?

My duties are completed. My Bible is highlighted. My radio is tuned to positive music. My friend group is solid and supportive. My laundry is … almost folded. I'm doing all the "right" things I think I should be doing to hang on to hope and stay on track with God's plan. I'm reading the Word, living the Word, and have learned to love the Word—and yet I experience the same old struggle.

And I find myself wondering, *What if we are just spinning our wheels?* Reading self-help books and devotionals, watching TED talks, praying heartfelt prayers to be made perfect …

What if we are working hard to get rid of (or hide) the very thing God wants to use for His glory?

Whitney had a tumultuous life. J. K. persevered through rejection and the fear of not publishing Harry Potter, and Marlee defied the odds to become a well-known actress, even though she was deaf. We don't recognize these individuals because of their great Christian faith (however, if I get the chance, I'll be sure to ask them if they know Jesus). But my point is, we consider these women to be worthwhile. If these women, whom we see as beautiful, successful, and accomplished, can live a worthwhile life even with their fears, faults, failures, and frailties, then how much more can we expect as women following Christ?

The motivational speeches that tell us we must overcome our fears, correct our faults, rise above our failures, and strengthen our frailties before we can be of any value sound inspiring at first. They sound right. Just look at the speakers—they have it all together, so surely we can do it too! But then we sit at home under piles of dishes and diapers or at our desks, staring at deadlines and dead ends and wonder: *How am I ever going to do all that? How am I supposed to make a success out of my mess?* And we might even wonder, *Even if I do all the work to get strong and fix my mistakes and overcome my weaknesses, will I be valued?*

Thankfully, God does not leave us alone with our thoughts. He's given us His Word, which is filled with examples of men and women He has used for His kingdom—people just like us. People like Moses. His life paints a different picture. It's a picture that shows it's possible to be:

- Faithful, even when we're afraid
- Included in God's plans, even with our faults
- Useful, even when we've failed
- Valuable, even when we feel damaged

God doesn't want to change what makes you, you. And about all those splinters that have fractured your faith? He accepts them—all of them. He accepts you, just as you are. Moreover, He wants to take that which has wrongly defined and misdirected you and use it to demonstrate how He can transform weakness to power, regret to purpose, and anxiety to peace.

He can transform weakness to power, regret to purpose, and anxiety to peace.

I'm thrilled you've chosen to journey with me to this place of healing and hope. And believe me, I know this will be well-traveled ground for some of you. I've been on this path myself many times before and revisit the frequented sod more often than I care to confess. After all, the idea that God can use us in our weakness is an old one—as old as the Bible itself!

But we can never have enough reminders of how God sees us, not as problems, but as His people. Broken and yet beautiful.

And this is not a book of empty encouragement that will leave you lost as to what to do next. It's not another motivating speech printed out on pages. I'm not going to tell you to pull up your boots or slap your own face or make lemonade from lemons. Instead, we'll dig into the story of Moses and see how, though God never fixed this man's faults or stopped him from his failures, He used him completely and fully for His glory. Every day after Moses heard God speaking through that burning bush was a day He spent following God—sometimes stumbling, tripping, or dragging, but following still. With a terrible past and an uncertain future, Moses was still able to put his trust in the God he knew. And that's what we can do today.

We'll also look at real-life examples from women I know who are staying faithful in the middle of struggles. These "Possibility Profiles" are not stories with happy-ever-after endings where everything has worked out exactly according to their plans, but stories in which these women are still living with, waiting on, and trusting in God to use them according to His plans.

We're going to move from possible outcomes to practical steps that help us see how God can use us. We are going to learn so much together. I can't wait! Now, let's go see what God can do, and meet Moses too.

Revealing My Potential

Use the next couple of pages to jot down your thoughts. (Remember, your thoughts matter!) Record your important ideas, precious pieces of revelation, and other significant snippets. Don't erase, edit, or omit. Just put pen or pencil to paper and listen to what God is trying to teach you through His Word.

How is your faith fractured?

In Romans 8:18, Paul wrote that "what we suffer now is nothing compared to the glory he will reveal to us later" (NLT). From where you stand right now, can you agree with Paul? (It's okay if your answer is no.) Why, or why not?

What if God's plan isn't to "fix" the things that have fractured your faith but instead to show His power through them, making your faith stronger than ever? What would that mean for you?

Chapter 1

What God Can Do

Can God do anything with me?

We could fill the pages of this book, and the pages of many books, telling of the things God can do. Perhaps the chapter titles would include: "Heal," "Provide," "Calm the Storm," "Protect," "Comfort," and "Deliver." It could be a collection of stories describing all the wonderful acts of God. What an encouraging book that would be! Maybe the cover would have a beautiful sunrise bursting through a thick cloud of fog, attempting to capture the glory of the Lord. Oh, I can see it now, resting on coffee tables everywhere!

Before we send this book to be published, let me ask a question. Would you be able to contribute a story to such a book? Or would the book be filled with stories of what God can do in the lives of other people? Do you believe God can do things in your life? That God can heal, can provide, can calm the storm? Or do you believe God can for *others* but not for you?

Do you believe God can for others but not for you?

Ouch, I just stepped on my own toes—are yours aching too?

In this chapter we are going to address this thorny question: Why do we believe God can do things for others but can't do anything for us? I've asked God for the bandwidth to help us understand why we have trouble believing He *can*, to teach us who He *is*, and to develop our confidence to believe He *will*.

Do I Believe?

There's really no gentle way to say this, so I'm going to rip the bandage right off the wound and get this conversation started: we can't believe a God we don't know. It's impossible to believe God *can* if we don't know who God *is*.

It's impossible to believe God can if we don't know who God is.

Please take note of what I *didn't* say. I did not say that we can't believe in a God we don't know yet. When people first believe in Jesus, they often come to Him with little knowledge and yet trust Him as their Savior. God seeks us: "For the Son of man has come to save that which was lost" (Matt. 18:11 NASB). He chooses us: "Even as he chose us in him before the foundation of the world, that we should be holy and blameless before him" (Eph. 1:4 ESV). It is through a daily commitment to our relationship with Him that we get to know Him. We read His Word, pray, and obey.

Jesus talks about this kind of believing. One day Jesus had a conversation with a Jewish leader who was amazed at all the miracles he had seen Jesus do. Nicodemus said to Jesus, "We know that you are a teacher who has come from God. For no one could perform the signs you are doing if God were not with him" (John 3:2). This Jewish leader had some knowledge of God but did not yet believe in Jesus as God. Jesus explained to Nicodemus that anyone could receive Him, even if they didn't *know* Him; they only had to believe.

> For God so loved the world that he gave his one and only Son, that whoever believes in him shall not perish but have eternal life. For God did not send his Son into the world to condemn the world, but to save the world through him. (John 3:16–17)

The apostle Paul also plainly explained salvation in his letter to the Romans:

> If you declare with your mouth, "Jesus is Lord," and believe in your heart that God raised him from the dead, you will be saved. For it is with your heart that you believe and are justified, and it is with your mouth that you profess your faith and are saved. (Rom. 10:9–10)

For the sake of your eternity, and the opportunity to *know* the God who *can do*, I pray that, if you have not yet taken that step to accept Jesus as your Savior, you will believe in Him and not perish, declare with your mouth that He is Lord, believe in your heart, and profess your faith. He longs for you to know Him and experience Him in your life. Salvation is the first step in believing that God *can do*.

Salvation is the first step in believing that God can do.

Even when we believe in God for our salvation and trust Him with our eternal future, it is not uncommon to have moments of unbelief. Yes, I said *not* uncommon. We may struggle with questions like these: Can salvation be that simple? Am I really saved? Can I really go to heaven after all the terrible things I've done? Does God find me useful for joining Him in His work?

Friend, if you have asked Jesus to come into your life and save you, then you are saved! Write the time and place down when you made this decision, if you haven't already done so. Celebrate it!

Our enemy, the devil (I hate even typing his name), wants to steal the joy and assurance of our faith and replace it with unbelief about everything God wants to do in and through our life. But there is no way he can steal our salvation: "I give them eternal life, and they shall never perish; no one will snatch them out of my hand" (John 10:28). Since he can't snatch us away, Satan desires to render us completely ineffective and unusable in God's kingdom, for His plan, and for His glory. We have to keep believing that God *can* even when He isn't at the moment.

We have to keep believing that God can even when He isn't at the moment.

In the Bible, the apostle Mark told of a time when a man brought his demon-possessed son to Jesus. The man said to Jesus, "If you can?" in regard to his son's healing. To which Jesus replied, "Everything is possible for one who believes." The boy's father exclaimed, "I do believe; help me overcome my unbelief!" (Mark 9:23–24). Did the man believe or not believe? We can be certain the man believed because he brought his son to Jesus to be healed (Mark 9:17). That being true, why did he cry out to Jesus to help his unbelief?

Apistía (ap-is-tee'-ah) is the Greek word for *unbelief* and means "weakness of faith" or "betraying a trust."[1] The father had faith, but in that moment, he realized the faith that had brought him to Jesus wasn't as strong as it should have been. One has to have faith in order to recognize a weakness of faith. Theologian Charles Spurgeon defined this concept as feeble faith, rather than faithless: "While men have no faith, they are unconscious of their unbelief, but as soon as they get a little faith, then they begin to be conscious of the greatness of their unbelief."[2]

Another way of saying this is that the man believed what Jesus could do for others but wasn't sure that Jesus could do the same thing for him and his son. Sound familiar?

We will have times in our faith adventure when we momentarily struggle to believe God's promises and have to fight to make His Word an anchor for our soul. This man was one of many in the Bible who were confronted with unbelief. The disciples wrestled with unbelief when people needed to be fed and they only had some fish and bread (John 6:1–15). When her brother died, Martha found it hard to believe that Jesus could do anything about Lazarus's death (11:38–44). We can't forget Thomas, who, after spending years with Jesus, seeing Him perform miracles, and hearing of the plans for His crucifixion and resurrection, had to touch the holes in Jesus's body before he would completely believe (20:24–29).

Wrestling with believing that God *can do* will strengthen our faith. However, when we allow unbelief to convince us He *can't do* or *won't do*, that's when our faith begins to fracture. Each individual mentioned above got real with Jesus about their doubt.

- The father: "I do believe; help me overcome my unbelief!" (Mark 9:24).
- The disciples: "But what good is that with this huge crowd?" (John 6:9 NLT).
- The sister: "If you had been here, my brother would not have died" (John 11:21).
- The disciple: "Unless I see the nail marks in his hands and put my finger where the nails were,

and put my hand into his side, I will not believe"
(John 20:25).

Jesus can handle our temporary uncertainty. God can handle
our tough questions. His Spirit will gracefully help us reconcile our
unbelief and realign our faith with the truth of His Word. He will
lead us to know who He is.

Jesus can handle our temporary uncertainty.

It is true: you can't really start knowing God until you believe
and receive Him as Savior. Once you believe *in* Him, you can truly
know Him. The joy of life is knowing Him and getting to know Him
better and better. Let's talk about that—knowing God. Who is this
God who *can do*? Oh, the possibilities are endless!

Scripture verifies, "For nothing will be impossible with God"
(Luke 1:37 ESV). All we have to do is believe and watch: "And without faith it is impossible to please God, because anyone who comes
to him must believe that he exists and that he rewards those who
earnestly seek him" (Heb. 11:6). The reward is in the seeking and
the knowing.

Who Is the God of Can?

The question has been asked and answered by thousands of experts
and theologians: Who is the God of *can*? So to attempt to breathe
fresh wind into such a hefty topic is a bit overwhelming. To be
completely honest, I feel less than qualified to address it. Who am I

that I can know God? After all, I'm only a wife and mother with an elementary education degree.

Maybe you've felt the same way. Perhaps you've believed the same lie—the "I'm only" lie.

Many years ago, I set out to know God—to know Him beyond my fill-in-the-blank Bible studies and devotionals. With Satan the liar's (John 8:44) fiery words of doubt breathing down my neck, I began reading the Bible, book by book, chapter by chapter, and word by word. With fresh eyes I read stories I had first learned while sitting in the teddy bear chairs of my kindergarten Sunday school class, sipping Hi-C orange drink and nibbling on saltine crackers. My teacher used the felt board to make the stories come to life. Hearing again of the creation, the ark, the tower of Babel, and of Joseph and his colorful coat drew me in like a moth to light. I paused over a word that changed me forever as I read about the exodus of God's people from Egypt.

Through His reluctant leader Moses, God said to the Israelites, "I will take you as my own people, and I will be your God. Then you will know that I am the LORD your God, who brought you out from under the yoke of the Egyptians" (Ex. 6:7). God wanted His people to *know* Him. Wow! In reading, I began to notice throughout the Old Testament that phrase, "know that I am the LORD God."

I was never one to pay attention to little, seemingly insignificant words. In fact, I had always struggled with reading as a child, and I often didn't pay attention to words—period. Reading through the Bible was a whole new experience for me. However, on this particular day, this particular word got my attention. Looking back, I'm certain this was God's whisper to my heart, inviting me to go deeper in my faith.

At the time, I wasn't sure how to dig deeper into the meaning of the word *know*. I was fairly certain it didn't mean the same in English as it did when it was recorded in Hebrew. After fumbling around in some free Bible study websites, I clicked on a link that took me to another link with the meaning of this word as written in Exodus 6:7. Through the word *yada* (yaw-dah'), God tells His people, "I want you to experience Me." *Yada* is an experiential knowledge of God. It means "doing life together with Him, allowing Him to lead the way while we obey and watch the miraculous happen." God wanted to be in relationship with His people then, and He still does today.

God wanted to be in relationship with His people then, and He still does today.

While the Old Testament is written primarily in Hebrew, the New Testament is written primarily in Greek. Therefore, the word for *know* is not the same in both testaments, but the definition paints the same picture. *Ginōskō* (ghin-oce'-ko) means "to become acquainted with."[3] Life experiences, joyous or sorrowful and difficult or delightful, are all ways to become acquainted with someone.

My friendship with my very best friend started in preschool when we were only five years old. Other than God, no one, not even my husband, is more acquainted with the nuances that make me, me. How is this possible? She has known me longer, and we have shared more gut-wrenching, heartbreaking, and belly-laughing moments than I have shared with anyone else I know. We have trusted each other with information we've never told another living soul. We have *experienced* life together, and those experiences have created a bond that doesn't compare to any other.

Just like my BFF wants to share life with me, the God who *can* wants us to share experiences with Him. Are you having trouble believing me? Okay, then believe Jesus. As Jesus prepared to die, He intimately prayed to His Father. He said, "This is eternal life, that they may know You, the only true God, and Jesus Christ whom You have sent" (John 17:3 NKJV). Underline or highlight the word *know*.

Even though I had connected these dots, I still struggled with the idea that God wanted me to know Him beyond knowing what He did for me on the cross. Determined to dig deeper and understand how to know God, I discovered something else: God had more than one name. I could know Him by His many names.

Wait a minute. Press pause. How had I missed this information in all my Bible-study-blank-filling-in and sermon-note-taking? The God of *can do* has other names. Maybe you know this information, or maybe this is your "wait a minute" moment too.

Experiencing life together is not the only way to know someone. It's very important to know the name, or in this case the names, of the person with whom you are sharing life. Another way to experientially know our great God is to call Him by name.

The names of God generally have two parts and begin with either *Yahweh* or *El*. Yahweh, also translated as Jehovah or LORD (notice the all caps), describes God's self-existence and enables us to peek into His character. *El*, which is the plural for Elohim, means "strong one" and is used when discussing God's sovereignty, creativity, and power.

We can know Him as:

- *Yahweh Tsidkenu*: The Lord my Righteousness. God is the source of my righteousness (Jer. 23:6).
- *Yahweh Jireh*: The Lord will provide. God makes provision for His people (Gen. 22:14).
- *Yahweh Maccaddeshcem*: The Lord is my Sanctifier. God forgives my sins and through His Spirit makes me holy, and sets me apart for His purposes (Ex. 31:13 ESV).
- *Yahweh Nissi*: The Lord is my Banner. God fights for His people; He is our victory (Ex. 17:15).
- *Yahweh Shammah*: The Lord is always there. God will never leave or forsake us (Ezek. 48:35).
- *Yahweh Rapha*: The Lord is my Healer. God is the one who heals (Ex. 15:26).
- *Yahweh-Rohi*: The Lord is my Shepherd. The Lord shepherds and cares (Ps. 23:1).
- *Yahweh Shalom*: The Lord is Peace. Our peace comes from God (Judg. 6:24).
- *Yahweh Sabaoth*: The Lord of Hosts. God is the commander of heaven's armies (1 Sam. 1:3 NKJV).

We can call Him:

- *El Shaddai*: God Almighty, who loves and comforts but also corrects and chastens. (Gen. 49:24).

- *El Elyon*: God Most High, who is strong, sovereign, and supreme (Job 42:2).
- *El Roi*: God Who Sees, the one who sees (Gen. 16:13).
- *El-Shaddai Rohi*: God Almighty; the mighty One is not like any other "god" (Gen. 17:1).
- *El Deah*: God of Knowledge; all wisdom comes from God (1 Sam. 2:3 NKJV).
- *El Olam*: The Everlasting God, who is unchangeable and inexhaustible (Gen. 21:33 NKJV).

Doesn't just seeing these names cover you with peace like a warm blanket on a cool night? Oh, it does me! I love every one of His names. One of my favorites is Yahweh Jireh (or Jehovah-Jireh), the Lord provides. I've witnessed His provision as I've prayed to Him, calling this name, and watched this name transform my husband's faith.

Not too long ago, and for the second time in a period of a few years, my husband, Scott, found himself without a job. Unemployment is hard on anyone, but especially hard on a man who has a family to support. I encouraged him with words, prayers, and Bible verses on his bathroom mirror. *God will take care of us. God has a plan for you. God sees what's going on. God has something better in store. God is faithful.*

Nothing I said or did seemed to make a difference. As hard as I tried, cried, and prayed, Scott remained jobless and his faith seem to wane. Sometimes God has to get us out of the way so He can work. After a weekend of ministry, I returned home to a husband who had been ministered to by the Holy Spirit. The conversation went something like this:

Scott: "Did you know that God's name is Jehovah-Jireh?"

Me: "Yes, I did."

Scott: "Do you know that it means 'God will provide'?"

Me: "Yes, I did. How did you find this out?"

Scott: "It was the lesson in Sunday school. God just assured me that He will provide for us."

Sweeter is the blessing to know and to experience Him by name.

Friends, Jehovah-Jireh hasn't failed us. Even when Scott found a job but the company closed and we faced another year of unemployment. During the seasons of having no work, Jehovah-Jireh provided ways for Scott to make money to take care of our family. The God Who Provides wrote a book in my heart and gave me the opportunity to put it on paper and have it published. Now our family tagline is "Jehovah-Jireh."

Each time we were afforded an occasion to work or receive payment for a service we rendered, we called His name. Over the door on the inside of Scott's office are tall vinyl letters spelling Jehovah-Jireh. He intentionally hung God's name there so he would see it from his office chair and constantly be reminded of God's faithfulness, even when His provision looks different from what we expect or is not on our timetable. Would God have provided for our needs even if I hadn't prayed His name of provision? Absolutely. Oh, but sweeter is the blessing to know and experience Him by name. Knowing Him through experience and by name opens our eyes to what He can do.

What God Can Do

Our knowledge of God's names and experiences with Him develop our confidence to believe He *can do*. Let's circle back around to the question that started our chapter: What can God do? Our initial responses might be: *Anything He wants. Everything, because He is all-powerful and all-knowing, and His presence is everywhere.* Maybe there would be more specific answers based on His names: *He can heal. He can save. He can sanctify. He can provide. He can protect.* These would all be correct answers. However, there's a tightrope we walk believing that He can and trying to understand why He doesn't. To help us maintain our balance, we need to revisit the name of God that speaks to the essence of this quandary.

El Elyon describes God as Most High; one who is strong, supreme, and sovereign. The sovereignty of God declares that He is in complete control over all things. And yet, people make real choices with real consequences, both favorable and unfavorable. Since both of these statements are true, we can deduce that God doesn't *cause* all things to happen, but He divinely *consents* to things taking place.

At first glance this might not seem fair. Why would a loving Father allow His children to make huge mistakes or be victims of a heinous act? You are probably nodding your head or even saying out loud, "What she said!" This can of worms has been opened and debated for many years by the best and brightest biblical scholars. God's sovereignty is supposed to be a comfort to us, not an issue to be concerned about or debated over. The truth is that God does not violate our wills by choosing us and redeeming us. Rather, He changes our hearts so that our wills choose Him. The Bible shows us that "we love Him because He first loved us" (1 John 4:19 NKJV) and "you did not choose me, but I chose you" (John 15:16 ESV).[4]

In regard to mistakes and wrong decisions, God has given us everything we need to wisely discern solutions to the problems we face. "His divine power has given us everything we need for a godly life through our knowledge of him who called us by his own glory and goodness" (2 Pet. 1:3). His Word is a book of instructions, full of wisdom and guidance. "All Scripture is inspired by God and profitable for teaching, for reproof, for correction, for training in righteousness; so that the man of God may be adequate, equipped for every good work" (2 Tim. 3:16–17 NASB). We fail to make good decisions when we don't consult the Word and submit to the Holy Spirit's work in our life.

El Elyon is stronger than our greatest weakness and higher than anything that seeks to bring us down.

As to the victimizing of individuals because of another's free will, there is not an easy answer. I could craft some comforting words, but the truth is, the cries of the innocent bewilder me. Scripture is full of individuals who suffered at the hands of the free will of others, starting when Cain killed Abel (Gen. 4:8). Joseph was sold into slavery by his brothers (Gen. 37:28), and Dinah (Gen. 34:2) and later Tamar were victims of sexual assault (2 Sam. 13:14). In the New Testament, John the Baptist was beheaded (Matt. 14:8–10), Paul was imprisoned (Acts 16:22–23), and Jesus was crucified (Matt. 27:32–37).

The truth is, on this side of heaven, no one will be able to give a satisfactory explanation to why innocent people suffer. We live in a fallen world, full of sinful people (including us), but we were saved for an eternal existence by a redeeming and just Father. He will satisfy all suffering and redeem all our pain. God's promise is clear, "And we know [with great confidence] that God [who is deeply concerned about us] causes all things to work together [as a plan] for good for those who love God, to those who are called according to His plan and purpose" (Rom. 8:28 AMP). Please notice the word *know*. It screamed *ginóskō* (ghin-oce'-ko) to me. In fact, I assumed it was the *ginóskō know*. Oh, but God—He breathed another word into this scripture, one of greater hope for the hurting and those who have been wrongly victimized at the hands of another.

This Greek word for *know* is *eidó*, short *e* (i'-do). *Helps Word Studies* breaks down the meaning like this—get ready, it is *so* good!— "('seeing that becomes knowing') then is a gateway to grasp spiritual truth (reality) from a physical plane … a physical seeing (sight) which should be the constant bridge to mental and spiritual seeing (comprehension)."[5]

God will make things all right, or help us be all right with things.

In the most simple explanation: God will make things all right, or help us be all right with things, and we will recognize His Spirit's work in doing so.

While making certain all the vile and wrong that happens works out for our good, He wants us to see a spiritual truth and constantly be working to comprehend all things surrounding the situation. In return, He calls us to love Him and live for His purpose. With a promise like this, and such powerful names, who wouldn't love and live for a God like that?

The sovereignty of God is indeed complex. Living under the sovereignty of God means believing He *can*, trusting He *will*, and accepting if He *doesn't*. His sovereignty is supreme and perfect, and we can rest in it. El Elyon is stronger than our biggest weakness and higher than anything that seeks to bring us down. Our fears, faults, failures, and frailties have no power over God's sovereign plan and purpose for our life, so we shouldn't permit them to have power over us. God won't allow anything to thwart His plan, and we shouldn't believe anything or anyone who tells us otherwise. "I know that You can do all things, and that no thought or purpose of Yours can be restrained or thwarted" (Job 42:2 AMPC).

Living under the sovereignty of God means believing He can, trusting He will, and accepting if He doesn't.

What Can God See in Me?

Earlier I shared that Jehovah-Jireh was one of my favorite names of God. Scott and I experienced God through this name. Another of my cherished names of God is El Roi, the God who sees. It overwhelms me to even consider that El Elyon, the supreme and sovereign One, sees me and that He also cares for me. No matter who you are or what you've done, God, the creator of the heavens and earth, cares about you. And what's more awesome is, the very first person to ever call Him El Roi was an Egyptian slave, a castoff from the crowd, and a woman who, by that day's standard, would be considered a nobody.

But she wasn't a nobody to God.

We meet this woman named Hagar in Genesis 16 when she is brought into the twisted saga of Abraham's wife, Sarah, who is desperate to have a child. God promised Abraham that he would father a child late in life and through that child all nations would be blessed. The *Reader's Digest* version of the story goes like this: Sarah became impatient for God's plan. (I can relate to you, Sarah-girl.) She made the hasty decision to let her husband sleep with her maidservant. (I can't relate to *that*! It's messed up on so many levels!) Hagar conceived and gave birth to Ishmael. Sarah got jealous (imagine that), mistreated Hagar, and Hagar ran away. Let's join up with Hagar near a spring in the desert on the road to Shur (Gen. 16:7), where she converses with the angel of the Lord.

God believes everyone is worthy of seeing.

The angel listens and speaks prophecy over her unborn child. Scripture references the conversation this way, "The LORD talked to Hagar." Hagar's response is priceless. "She began to use a new name for God. She said to him, 'You are "God Who Sees Me."' She said this because she thought, 'I see that even in this place God sees me and cares for me!'" (Gen. 16:13 ERV).

God believes everyone is worthy of seeing. He sees in us what no one else can: a *worthwhile possibility*.

God is El Roi, the God who sees. He sees our fears. He sees our faults. He sees our failures and frailties. We see them too, but unlike God, we allow these deficiencies to hold us back from walking out the call God has for our life. Hagar failed. She was part of a scheme that interrupted her life, but she didn't wreck God's plan. (Remember: His plans won't be thwarted, no matter how royally we mess up.) God wants to use our weaknesses to strengthen us, rather than weigh us down.

God sees in us what no one else can: a worthwhile possibility.

The word *potential* can be defined as "present but not yet visible, apparent, or actualized, excellence or ability that may or may not be developed; possible, as opposed to actual." A person with potential is someone who is a worthwhile possibility. Despite our fears, faults, failures, and frailties, God sees all His children through the same lens, the lens of potential. Our potential is present, but may not be visible; possible, but may not be actual. In Christ we are a worthwhile possibility.

God *can* see our potential even when we can't. Moses is another excellent example of an individual who had possibility but allowed the weight of his past to keep him from seeing the impact his future could have in the kingdom of God. God had big plans for Moses's life. He was destined to be the leader of God's people; to lead them out of a life of slavery in Egypt and into a life of abundance in the Promised Land of Canaan. He would be the communicator of God's law to God's people and the author of the Pentateuch (the first five books of the Bible). Big plans, I tell you.

God wants to use our weaknesses to strengthen us, rather than weigh us down.

Moses entered the world with a death sentence on his life. The Israelites, even though subjected to cruel slavery, were faithfully prolific. As their numbers increased, so did Pharaoh's insecurity. His attempt to work them harder didn't stop the pitter-patter of Israelite baby feet, but he came up with a plan that would. Pharaoh gave this order: "Every Hebrew boy that is born you must throw into the Nile, but let every girl live" (Ex. 1:22). *But man's plan can't thwart God's plan.* God has given man free will, but ultimately, our choices will be worked out to be in alignment with God's plan.

Moses was born, and in an attempt to save her child, Moses's mother placed him in a basket and set the basket in the Nile River. The Nile just happened to be where Pharaoh's daughter would go to bathe. She found Moses and adopted him as her own. Moses grew up in Egypt, the very place he would eventually fulfill God's plan for his life, but not before an epic fail. However, we have a lot of his life to examine before then.

As first, Moses didn't see himself as a worthwhile possibility. In the following chapters, we will closely examine his arguments with God about the calling on his life. Eventually, Moses surrendered his fears, faults, failures, and frailties and lived the life God planned for him.

Do you struggle to believe that God sees you as a person with potential?

He is the God who *can do* and the God who sees. He saw the first drink you ever took. He knows when you went to the clinic and cried the entire time. He sees the links you click and the person you spend time with (who is not your spouse). He sees you crying in the pillow as you process your overspending. He knows that you have to sleep with the light on. He sees you standing in the unemployment line after losing another job. Maybe today you are like Hagar, feeling like a castoff, camped out in the desert region of Shur, wondering, *Does God even see me?*

Oh, my sweet friend, may I hold your beautiful face in my hands and lean in real close to speak truth? He sees your potential and believes you are a worthwhile possibility. You were destined for a great plan, "for we are His workmanship [His own master work, a work of art], created in Christ Jesus [reborn from above—spiritually transformed, renewed, ready to be used] for good works, which God prepared [for us] beforehand [taking paths which He set], so that we would walk in them [living the good life which He prearranged and made ready for us]" (Eph. 2:10 AMP).

God sees your potential and believes you are a worthwhile possibility.

God determines your destiny. Don't allow your fears, faults, failures, and frailties to derail you from His plan. He has saved you and called you to a holy life—not because of anything you have done, but because of His own purpose and grace, grace given to you in Christ Jesus before the beginning of time (2 Tim. 1:9).

Reflecting on What God Can Do

1. I remember reading Genesis 1:1 when I was little, "In the beginning God created the heavens and the earth." Little-girl me was blown away by a God so big, who could create everything. What Bible stories have you read, or even just heard about, that have shaped your idea of who God is in a significant way?

2. In this chapter, I shared a couple of my favorite names of God. Now it's your turn. Choose two names of God that stand out to you. What do those names mean to you? Select a name that's new to you, and pray this week to God using that new name.

3. I have a skin condition call rosacea, and the thought of someone seeing me without makeup unnerves me. But God doesn't care about my complexion. God sees me. God sees you. You are never alone, and God is a come-as-you-are God. What do you feel when you think about the fact that God sees who you are?

4. Sometimes I wonder what in the world God was thinking when He chose me to serve Him through speaking and writing. Moses also did not consider himself worthy to be God's messenger. Yet he led the Israelites out of their suffering in Egypt and saw God face to face. What does that tell you about what God can do?

5. Our looks or abilities are of no concern to God. Turn in your Bible to Proverbs 31:30. What kind of women will be praised? Turn to 1 Samuel 16:7. What does God look at when He looks at you? Write a short prayer to God in response to these two scriptures.

Revealing My Potential

Use the space provided to respond to this prompt: "You are a worthwhile possibility." What do those words mean to you?

Chapter 2

What God Can Do through My Failures

Am I still useful after I've failed?

*Failure: something we attempt to
do but fail to accomplish.*

In Exodus 2, Moses's life took a turn for the worse when he took the life of an Egyptian soldier. It was a rash move, a horrible crime, and a moral failure for this man who had been raised as royalty. Murder was an offense punishable by death.

Maybe your failure isn't as extreme as that of Moses. (I hope not!) However, the weight of failure can make you feel weak in faith and stagnant in your spiritual life, unable to advance in your relationship with God or your relationship with others.

Author, salesman, and motivational speaker Zig Ziglar encouraged people to "remember that failure is an event, not a person." We often allow failure, no matter how insignificant, to define and direct our future. Moses's life teaches us that failure may fracture our faith, but it doesn't have to destroy it.

Failure may fracture our faith, but it doesn't have to destroy it.

You may have experienced a bit of whiplash as you flipped the page to start this chapter—moving from the pep talk about potential to the weighty word of *failure*. The turn might have been too sharp. Maybe your mind is filled with flashbacks. Like the news ticker crawling across the bottom of your television screen, your failures scroll through your mind. I can see mine clearly: I'm transported back to the time I had to take the National Teacher's Exam three times, but then barely passed. Or the time I wore new white Keds during the Easter Cantata, thinking, *It's dark and my choir robe will cover my feet.* Or the time I tried out for the solo, but someone else was selected.

The plain and simple fact is, nobody wants to fail, but everybody does. It's our response to the failure that matters.

For some reason, some Christians are under the misconception that we will be sheltered from failure, when in reality the only shelter we can count on is the One in whom we can take refuge when we do fail. "Whoever dwells in the shelter of the Most High will rest in the shadow of the Almighty" (Ps. 91:1). Yes, as unfair as it seems, in this world we will have troubles. From the mouth of Jesus we hear this: "I have told you all this so that you may have peace in me. Here on earth you will have many trials and sorrows. But take heart, because I have overcome the world" (John 16:33 NLT).

It's our response to failure that matters.

Failure doesn't discriminate; everyone everywhere fails. Regardless of your account balance at the bank, standing in the community, position in the company, or diplomas on the wall, you will fail. I realize this news doesn't make you want to stand on the table and do your best Jesus jig, but friends tell each other the truth, even when the truth is hard to hear. Friends also help each other deal with and rise above failure. They stand with each other offering prayer, godly counsel, biblical support, chocolate, and maybe even a day of Netflix bingeing.

Oh, how I wish we could curl up in the new snuggly throws I bought on clearance with stacked coupons, sit on the sectional in my family room, share some chocolate (dark is my preference), discuss spiritual truths, and watch a sappy, old, black-and-white movie. Yes! That would be the ideal way to process such a heavy subject, but alas, that isn't possible, so we will have to pretend.

Let's talk about Moses, his failures (yes, plural), and how he dealt with them. For a moment, he almost let them define and defeat him. But God—perhaps two of the best words in the Bible (they can turn a story on a dime)—didn't allow Moses's failure to wreck his potential. In fact, God knew exactly how Moses would fail and still chose him to be the leader of His people. Now that is mind blowing. *God knows ahead of time what wrong we will do yet still chooses us to participate in His kingdom work.*

Drop the mic.

You may think your life has been wrecked by failure. However, God knew exactly how you would fail. He has assignments for you that only you can do. Your failure has not disqualified you from His plan or decreased your potential. In fact, we will learn that failure is a great teacher. And when we respond to it correctly, it can be a powerful tool in our arsenal against our enemy.

> **Your failure has not disqualified you from His plan or decreased your potential.**

Although failure is inevitable and all-inclusive, we aren't destined to live in an uncertain cycle of disappointment. Failure can be a powerful force in our life, but not more powerful than our God. Failure can't define who we are or defeat who we can become. No matter how often we fail, we are still useful to God.

Picking Up Where We Left Off

We last saw Moses being lifted from a basket among the papyrus reeds of the Nile River. As the sovereignty of God would have it, this boy was born with a royal death sentence, "Then Pharaoh gave this order to all his people: 'Every Hebrew boy that is born you must throw into the Nile, but let every girl live'" (Ex. 1:22). Yet this Hebrew boy was born, saved by midwives, hidden by his mother, floated on a river, and plucked out of the water by the princess of the land. Then he was given back to his mother to be nursed and raised until he was older and could live in the palace with his adopted mother, the daughter of Pharaoh. How's that for a life-insurance policy?

> Pharaoh's daughter said to her, "Take this baby and nurse
> him for me, and I will pay you." So the woman took the
> baby and nursed him. When the child grew older, she took
> him to Pharaoh's daughter and he became her son. She
> named him Moses, saying, "I drew him out of the water."
> (Ex. 2:9–10)

Moses was permitted not only to live but to live with his mother among his own people—the Hebrews. This fostered a love for his people, which became especially helpful later (spoiler alert) when he was leading them out of bondage to the Land of Promise. Yes, it was all working out just like a godly hero's story should go.

Until …

Maybe you can identify. Your life hasn't been easy, but you've received blessings. You've sensed God near, guiding and caring for you. Then one day, you royally mess up. And all the dreams and hopes and plans you had visions of suddenly seem to disappear like the morning mist on the Nile.

> One day, after Moses had grown up, he went out to where
> his own people were and watched them at their hard labor.

He saw an Egyptian beating a Hebrew, one of his own people. Looking this way and that and seeing no one, he killed the Egyptian and hid him in the sand. (Ex. 2:11–12)

"Looking this way and that." This was a deliberate killing. This was not self-defense. This was not an accident. This was a purposeful act, committed (most likely) in a rage. This was a failure of epic proportion. The taking of another person's life is murder. Though all failure isn't sin, this particular failure is definitely a sin.

You might be squirming in your seat right now, maybe adjusting yourself a bit as you read the word *murder*. Please know that I'm not throwing the *m*-word around casually, without heart. I have an acute sensitivity to the subject because I knew someone who was murdered in the first degree. Moses's murder of this Egyptian was both a failure and a sin.

Let's park here for a few minutes to dialogue about failure and sin. Sin is always a failure, but failure isn't always a sin. Both sin and failure are redeemable, as well as forgivable. Our enemy will use both to separate us from God, cripple our faith, and custom-fit us with an "I'm no longer qualified to serve God" coat. This coat will not provide warmth, but instead will smother us with shame, douse us with doubt, and squelch our self-esteem. Satan's goal is to keep us stifled by failure so that we are unable to fulfill the calling God has on our life. And if we don't know how to separate failure and sin, he will have an even easier time being successful, because, as we've noticed, we all experience failures on a pretty regular basis.

Though the effects of both are similar, there is one obvious difference in the two. Sin requires forgiveness from God; failure does not, unless prompted by the Spirit. It's for this reason that we should completely examine ourselves through the light of God's Word and pray to let the Holy Spirit identify our sin. This must be resolved before we can process our failure in a healthy and productive way.

Sin is always a failure, but failure isn't always a sin.

While we are hard pressed, working toward our goal, it's easy to blur the lines between right and wrong. Sometimes in our zeal for success we inadvertently violate God's ways. Often, without intention, we hurt other people. Our motives may be pure as we set out to pursue our objective, yet pressure gets the best of us, expectations loom over us, and in haste we make poor choices that jeopardize our relationship with God as well as with those we love. When failure occurs, we look back and see the mess we left in our wake.

Though Moses's heart was in the right place (protecting his people), his mind was not. In this moment of anger, Moses impulsively violated God's law (established in stone later as "You shall not murder," Ex. 20:13). He set out to achieve justice—but his failure came in taking justice into his own hands, with no real thought or plan or wisdom. He did not ask for God's advice. He did not ask for anyone's advice. He just saw a problem and got rid of the problem. But in doing so, he took a human being's life. Moses could have brought the Egyptian before the courts. Being the adopted son of the princess of Egypt, he would have had some power. But instead, he took it upon himself to become judge, jury, and executioner. His own actions show he knew it was wrong. He tried to hide his deed. But our sins have a way of revealing themselves.

How Can We Know?

Taking the litmus test for recognizing sin in failure isn't exactly fun; however, it is necessary. We have to distinguish sin and failure in order to deal with them correctly. Otherwise our potential will be hidden, and this is exactly how the enemy wants us—pent up from fulfilling our potential by a wall of unresolved failures.

But unlike the tests we took while in school, we can invite a friend, an adviser, to assist us with this one. The Holy Spirit is our Helper, Teacher, Advocate, and Adviser. He also has the responsibility of convicting the world of sin. "And when He comes, He will convict and convince the world and bring demonstration to it about sin and about righteousness (uprightness of heart and right standing with God) and about judgment" (John 16:8 AMPC). In the aftermath of failure, it's crucial we spend time with the Holy Spirit, ask some tough questions, and wait for the answers. Here are some of the questions we can ask:

1. What all have I done wrong? Show me where I went wrong or how I sinned (Job 13:23).
2. How have I offended God or others? (Job 13:23).
3. Test me, God. Are my motives and desires good? (Ps. 26:2).
4. When did I deliberately not do what was good, and did I know what was good? (James 4:17).

I'll admit, this isn't easy, but God is so very faithful. He will hear our questions and tenderly respond to them with grace and mercy.

He is for us, not against us. God desires for us to move forward and not only believe we are a worthwhile possibility but to live like we believe it.

God is for us, not against us.

Forgiveness is the gateway to moving away from sin, working through our failure, and actualizing our potential. If God reveals any sin, our correct response is confession. We can consider David's prayer of admission as an example of how to humble ourselves before God and take responsibility for what we have done wrong.

> God, be merciful to me
> > because of your faithful love.
> Because of your great compassion,
> > erase all the wrongs I have done.
> Scrub away my guilt.
> > Wash me clean from my sin.
> I know I have done wrong.
> > I remember that sin all the time.
> I did what you said is wrong.
> > You are the one I have sinned against.
> I say this so that people will know
> > that I am wrong and you are right.
> > What you decided is fair.
> I was born to do wrong,
> > a sinner before I left my mother's womb.
> You want me to be completely loyal,
> > so put true wisdom deep inside of me.

Remove my sin and make me pure.
  Wash me until I am whiter than snow!
Let me hear sounds of joy and happiness again.
  Let the bones you crushed be happy again.
Don't look at my sins.
  Erase them all.
God, create a pure heart in me,
  and make my spirit strong again.
Don't push me away
  or take your Holy Spirit from me.
Your help made me so happy.
  Give me that joy again.
  Make my spirit strong and ready to obey you.
    (Ps. 51:1–12 ERV)

The Spirit convicts. We confess. God forgives, but that is not
the end. After we confess our sin to God and are reconciled, or
made right in Him, then we should also reconcile with those individuals who may have gotten hurt in our pursuit of our desires,
either intentionally or unintentionally. "If it is possible, as far as
it depends on you, live at peace with everyone" (Rom. 12:18). We
can't be at peace with and process our failure if we aren't living in
peace with others.

This short section should have come with a warning. As you
make peace with God and with others, the enemy will be hotter
than a firecracker on the Fourth of July that you have discovered
the freedom found in confession and forgiveness. He will take his
game plan for your life to a new level. Yes, the enemy has a plan for

your life too (Eph. 6:11), and you can be certain it doesn't include revealing your potential or helping you live out your calling. No, the prince of darkness wants us to stay depressed, oppressed, and stuck in the past, completely ignoring that we are a worthwhile possibility and useful to the kingdom of God.

Now that we can separate sin from failure, let's adjust our blankets, grab another piece of chocolate, and keep going as we learn how to process failure in a healthy and productive way.

When Failure Wants to Define Me

Failure is a word no one wants to be associated with. Let's be honest, many of us still cringe at the letter *F* because we have flashbacks of how it looked on the top right-hand corner of the composition paper we wrote about Abraham Lincoln. The red Bic felt-tip ink just made it worse, as if that *F* were shouting, "You are stupid! *You* are a failure!" Whether it comes with the memory of an Algebra II midterm (why, oh why, did they have to put letters with numbers?), a job interview, bankruptcy, a pregnancy test, or a divorce, the weight of this *f*-word can be heavy. Because no matter whether the failure was a sin or not, and no matter whether we really had much control over our success or not, the pain of failure is hard to overcome. The debris of the aftermath might take years to clean up.

Failure does not disqualify us from our potential.

However, the fact remains, *failure does not disqualify us from our potential.* If you haven't underlined that yet, do so now. We all fail, but we aren't a failure unless we allow failure to define us.

What or who defines you? Take a minute or longer if you need to. The quick Sunday school answer is God, right? We can just start quoting some bits of biblical descriptions that we are *supposed* to believe about ourselves, if that makes you feel better.

- Fearfully and wonderfully made (Ps. 139:14)
- A new creation (2 Cor. 5:17)
- Accepted (Rom. 8:1)
- Forgiven (1 John 1:9)
- Holy and dearly loved (Col. 3:12)

There's more we can add to the list, but you get my point. And do you feel better? Maybe … maybe not. If you are dealing with the fallout from failure right now, those words are probably not making the way through your dark mood yet.

We aren't a failure unless we allow failure to define us.

Now, if we are women following Christ, we are supposed to allow God's truth to define who we are. But do we? On good days, yes. When the sky is blue and the clouds are shaped like carousel ponies, when our boss sang our praises at the weekly staff meeting, when we cleaned our house from top to bottom in one day, when the laundry basket is finally empty, and dinner, all four courses, are ready for our people at the dot of 6:00 p.m. Yes, that is when we believe God's definition of who we are.

But what about the other days, the days when none of that happens? Who defines you then?

Parents. Past. Unruly children. Finances. Friends. Social media. Print media. The boss. The crotchety coworker. An abusive partner. Education. Possessions. Property. Success … or failure.

Earlier we talked in depth about the importance of believing God can. Well, we also have to believe what God says that *we can* do and what He says about who *we are*. Ask yourself this: Why is it easier to believe that words like *chosen, not forsaken, forgiven, accepted,* and the like apply to that other woman over there but not to you? Has she never failed?

Our failure is not more powerful than our God.

This takes me back to the introduction to this book: Remember how we compare our insides to another's outside to determine our value and sum up our potential? If this doesn't change, we will constantly be getting in God's way of using our failures to empower our potential. He is more than capable of taking what we messed up, turning it upside down, twisting it sideways, and making it work for our good and His ultimate glory. But if we don't believe what He says, we may completely miss out on seeing Him work through us. Not even my failure, no matter how great, can redirect God's plan for me. "The LORD of Heaven's Armies has spoken— who can change his plans? When his hand is raised, who can stop him?" (Isa. 14:27 NLT). Our failure is not more powerful than our God. Let this truth define you.

Once you were alienated and hostile in your minds because of your evil actions. But now He has reconciled you by

His physical body through His death, to present you holy, faultless, and blameless before Him. (Col. 1:21–22 HCSB)

Are you feeling more like doing a Jesus jig yet? That is shoutin' news right there! If God, through the sacrifice of Jesus, has already reconciled us so we can now be presented as holy, faultless, and blameless, why should we allow our failures to define and defeat us? If God can redeem humanity's worst, sinful failures, can't He redeem that lost job or that messed-up freshman year or that embarrassing slip of the tongue? Are we really going to say that Jesus died for every murderer and adulterer and thief, and we can accept His salvation for all of that, but we're going to let His gift of grace get smothered by one bad day, or even one bad decade?

Experiencing failure doesn't make you a failure.

Experiencing failure doesn't make you a failure. Let's say that again: Experiencing failure doesn't make you a failure. We have all failed and fallen short of our own expectations (and the expectations of others). And you know what? We are in good company.

- Abraham should have trusted the Lord during the drought, but instead, in fear, he fled to Egypt (Gen. 12).
- Moses should have spoken to the rock to bring water, but instead he struck the rock twice (Num. 20).

- David should have gone out to war with his army, but instead he stayed at home and committed adultery (2 Sam. 11).
- Peter should have stood with Jesus in His final moments, but instead Peter denied Him three times (Matt. 26).

Paul gave the church of Colossae further words on the concept of living faultless—without failing. "But you must continue to believe this truth and stand firmly in it. Don't drift away from the assurance you received when you heard the Good News" (Col. 1:23 NLT). "Continue" suggests an ongoing process, to keep on. When the winds of failure cause you to drift, fan the fire of your belief, stand firmly on the truth you know. Nothing you have done or will do can keep you from being in the presence of God. Nothing that you have done or will do will erase the potential God sees in you. You are a worthwhile possibility!

You are a worthwhile possibility!

When I Get to Defeat Failure

Defining who we are is the first step in processing failure in a healthy way. We can't allow a little pesky thing like failure hold us back from reaching our potential. Even when we *know* that we aren't a failure, it's still possible to allow the event to be a stumbling block to the future

God has planned for us. We have the power to defeat failure and shorten our stay in the aftermath if we respond appropriately to God.

There are various ways to react to failure, some better than others. Responding rightly isn't always simple; however, it is what God expects. We are women with potential, worthwhile in the eyes of God and confident of His love. We don't have to recoil in the face of failure. The truth is, failure is a great teacher; we just have to be willing to learn the lessons. Grab another piece of chocolate (oh, go ahead, it's the healthy kind), and let's mull over how to manage our reactions to failure.

> Repent, then, and turn to God, so that your sins may be wiped out, that times of refreshing may come from the Lord. (Acts 3:19)

Here's reaction number 1: *Deny—act as if it never happened.* Have you ever met "I Don't Know," "Not Me," or "Somebody"? They used to live at my house when my children were young. Funny thing, I never saw them, but I knew they were there. Whenever something got broken, "I Don't Know" did it. "Somebody" always left a mess in the kitchen after I cleaned it up. And that "Not Me" would never put the DVDs back in the cases.

Let's be real, the mom always knows, or will eventually find out who is responsible for the wrongdoing. Life can get complicated living in the land of denial. And isn't denial really just a way of lying? My children knew I'd rather have children who did something wrong than children who were liars. It is always right to tell the truth, own up to the mistake, and be part of the repair.

Make every effort to live in peace with everyone and to be holy; without holiness no one will see the Lord. (Heb. 12:14)

Failure reaction number 2: *Debug—act quickly to fix the situation or at the very least minimize the effects.* Debugging is something adults do well. With all our sophistication and keen reasoning skills, we conclude, "If I fix it, and quickly clean up the mess, then no one will ever find out." And you know what? It's quite possible that no one *will* ever know, but is that a right response? I'm not suggesting we leave the mess for someone else. The correct response is to push your glasses up on your nose, straighten your skirt, and face those involved with the truth as well as with solutions.

Whoever conceals their sins does not prosper, but the one who confesses and renounces them finds mercy. (Prov. 28:13)

Failure reaction number 3: *Dart—flee to Midian.* You may not be able to locate Midian on a map, but you've been there … the place you flee to when you don't want anyone to know you failed. Midian might be a favorite coffee shop, an outlet mall, or a screened-in porch at your BFF's house. It's okay to visit Midian, as long as you plan to return and face your failure. Moses fled to Midian after he was confronted with the murder of the Egyptian soldier; however, we never see in Scripture where he dealt with that sin.

Midian might be a favorite coffee shop, an outlet mall, or a screened-in porch at your BFF's house.

The next day he went out and saw two Hebrews fighting. He asked the one in the wrong, "Why are you hitting your fellow Hebrew?"

The man said, "Who made you ruler and judge over us? Are you thinking of killing me as you killed the Egyptian?" Then Moses was afraid and thought, "What I did must have become known."

When Pharaoh heard of this, he tried to kill Moses, but Moses fled from Pharaoh and went to live in Midian, where he sat down by a well. (Ex. 2:13–15)

Moses's failure not only took the life of another human, but it took away his standing with the Hebrew people as well. In an instant, the life he knew changed forever. His life was in danger, so he ran from Egypt. We have no way of knowing if Moses was going to use his time in Midian for personal reflection and spiritual development. It isn't clear whether he had plans to return to Egypt to face his failure. From what Scripture reveals, he was setting up house far from Egypt, his people, and his failure. But rest assured, God knew where Midian was and how to reach Moses.

Moses agreed to stay with the man, who gave his daughter Zipporah to Moses in marriage. Zipporah gave birth to a son, and Moses named him Gershom, saying, "I have become a foreigner in a foreign land." (Ex. 2:21–22)

We often let our failures push us away from the ones we love, to a place where we no longer feel like a worthwhile possibility full of potential. Maybe your Midian isn't a physical place but a way of living. The walls you've built around your heart keep others out. You've isolated yourself socially so no one will know anything about you or your past.

There is something God wants us to know, and a place He wants us to go, where only a failure can take us.

Midian can be lonely, but it can also be a place to learn from your failure, develop your relationship with God, hear from Him about His plans for you, and have your hidden potential revealed. God sovereignly permits failure. There is something He wants us to know, and a place He wants us to go where only a failure can take us. Midian can be a place of great discovery and healing. And you can rest assured, God knows where Midian is and how to reach you.

Meeting God in Midian

Midian is the place where everything changed for Moses. In the forty years away from the prestige of palace life, Moses was humbled. I suppose tending to dirty, smelly sheep would have that effect on anyone. The Bible doesn't record specific conversations between God and Moses about the murder, but we know that something changed. In all those years of inhaling dust, herding sheep, fighting off wild animals, and sleeping under the stars, Moses had some alone time with God. The time must have been good for his soul.

The evidence of his change is seen in God's calling. *Moses, you are now ready for your assignment. You failed. You sinned, but you have proven yourself faithful and ready. These forty years have been time well invested.* Okay, in my mind that is how the conversation went. Here's how the call actually came:

There the angel of the LORD appeared to him in flames of fire from within a bush. Moses saw that though the bush was on fire it did not burn up. So Moses thought, "I will go over and see this strange sight—why the bush does not burn up."

When the LORD saw that he had gone over to look, God called to him from within the bush, "Moses! Moses!"

And Moses said, "Here I am." (Ex. 3:2–4)

The LORD said, "I have indeed seen the misery of my people in Egypt. I have heard them crying out because of their slave drivers, and I am concerned about their suffering." (Ex. 3:7)

So now, go. I am sending you to Pharaoh to bring my people the Israelites out of Egypt. (Ex. 3:10)

On one hand, our time in our "Midian" is when we can discover all failure isn't bad or destructive, that things don't work out sometimes and that's okay. The outcome is, *It ain't no big thing.* Our momentary failure is most likely not catastrophic, just a casualty of living in a sin-soaked world. We pick ourselves up, dust off the inconvenience, and learn not to treat every failure like it is the end of the world.

But Midian can also be a place where everything can change for us. Failure can be redeemed, fellowship with God can be restored, and our hurting heart can be repaired. We can spend quiet time with

God, reading His Word and granting the Spirit access to our heart. Prayers can be genuine and earnest. This is where we can humble ourselves and allow Him to lift us up. "The LORD upholds all who fall and lifts up all who are bowed down" (Ps. 145:14). We can discover that failure is only a detour, not a permanent place to reside.

Failure has value. It won't seem that way at first. The realization of failure stings. You really have to look for the value and be willing to wait for God to reveal it. Moses worked for his father-in-law for forty years, and all the while God knew of Moses's potential. God was waiting for just the right time to make it actual. In the meantime, Moses hung out with God and allowed his faith to mature.

Failure has value.

James, the brother of Jesus, speaks of the maturing of our faith. If you have read this scripture before, please don't brush over it. And I just love the Easy-to-Read Version's translation of these verses:

> You know that when your faith is tested, you learn to be patient in suffering. If you let that patience work in you, the end result will be good. You will be mature and complete. You will be all that God wants you to be. (James 1:3–4 ERV)

Waiting for the good to come and your faith to mature in the wake of failure is extremely difficult. Many moons ago, God birthed a dream in my heart to write a book. I had some experience in writing through the *Encouragement for Today* daily devotions with Proverbs 31 Ministries. Many other writers on the team were authoring books, and since I felt God's affirmation, I pursued publishing as well.

Friends, it never occurred to me that I would fail. My spirit stirred with God's approval. I was writing on a monthly basis for an international ministry, my speaking schedule was full, and my social media influence was strong. For anyone else, this was the perfect prescription for a publisher's nod. For anyone … except me (or so it seemed at the time). Each time I sat at the publisher's table to propose my book, I failed. And each time one of my friends' books was published, I was reminded of my failure.

Failure may fracture our faith, but it doesn't have to destroy it.

You've been there; I know you have. The degree hanging on your wall and years of experience with the company say you're qualified for the assignment, and your boss calls and gives the account to you. For months you invest all your nights and weekends in the big presentation. The idea is new, fresh, innovative, and rather edgy.

Presentation day comes, all the important people gather around the large glass table in the conference room with their steaming hot Styrofoam cups, and everyone waits with great anticipation to hear your proposal. Each person follows the presentation in their own folder with copies you made, in color and collated. Using the laser-pointer thingy, you confidently go through every point and move from slide to slide without missing a beat. You nail it.

In *your* head, you nailed it.

But, you didn't. Later that day the boss comes to your office and closes the door. The important people weren't that impressed. And neither was your boss.

God uses every failure to mature our faith.

God uses every failure to mature our faith, just like James said. Every minute of every day, every day of every month, and every year in Midian is part of preparing us for the big reveal; the moment when God unveils your potential and says, *You are ready for your assignment. You failed, but it's time to move on. You have potential and are a worthwhile possibility. I've known it all along, since you were born. I've got plans for you, girl, and had to bring you here to take you there.*

Failure may fracture our faith, but it doesn't have to destroy it.

File It Away for Safe Keeping

The key is *not* to avoid failing. That's impossible. But we want to be women who fail with grace and learn, so when we fail again, we will be wiser and well equipped to recover in spiritual style, and perhaps come to the aid of a friend who needs a hand.

We want to be women who fail with grace.

God is bigger than our failure. Name it. Learn from it. File it. Walk away and don't look back. The apostle Paul suggested the same thing: "One thing I do, forgetting those things which are behind and reaching forward to those things which are ahead" (Phil. 3:13 NKJV). Keep failure in the right perspective: failing doesn't mean you are a failure. The morning after a fire that destroyed his lab and all of his research, Thomas Edison said, "There is great value in disaster. All our mistakes are burned up. Thank God we can start anew." Think of it—he said that while he could still literally stand in the ashes of his failure. He delivered his first phonograph three weeks later.[1]

Thomas Edison didn't have to become a success before revealing his potential. He didn't have to even clean up his mess before he saw the good in the soot. And you don't have to either. Even if you are standing on the ashes of your failure right now, God sees you. And God wants to use you. Use failure as a marker on your spiritual timeline rather than letting it stall your faith journey. You are a worthwhile possibility full of potential. Don't stop now!

Moses's life teaches us that failure may fracture our faith, but it doesn't have to destroy it. One of the most powerful moments of failure is putting it in its place, behind us. Knowing who we are in the light of God's Word gives us the strength to clean up the debris and move on.

Reflecting on What God Can Do with My Failure

1. One of my favorite things about reading and studying God's Word is the discovery that God has a plan for everyone, even those who mess up. Moses is one of those guys. What was Moses's first big failure? Why did he fail?

2. My soul shudders when I consider my life, chapter and verse, left for all the world to read, especially my failures. I don't want to air my dirty laundry out for others to see. Think about a time you experienced failure that others could see. What was that like?

3. Jesus said, "I have told you all this so that you may have peace in me. Here on earth you will have many trials and sorrows. But take heart, because I have overcome the world" (John 16:33 NLT). The Greek word for *overcome* is *nikaó* (nik-ah'-o). It means "to deprive it of power to harm, to subvert its influence."[2] Failure doesn't have to influence us or our future. With God in us, we have the power to deny failure's power over us. How does this truth help you deal with the failure you have experienced?

4. Moses fled to Midian, hoping to hide from his failure and remain unknown. What happened there instead? What does that tell you about how God sees our failures?

5. Where is your "Midian"? Where can you go to learn from your failure and listen to God's voice?

Revealing My Potential

Use the space provided to respond to this prompt: What has God revealed to you about failure? What is one failure that is hanging over you and holding you back from being the person God created you to be?

_____

_____

_____

Possibility Profile: Sharon

The two-book contract with the publisher was a gift from the Lord and was a dose of oxygen and refreshment to my soul. Having just endured a long season of trial in an area of my personal life, receiving the book offer from an enthusiastic publisher seemed like God whispering to me, *I see you. I was with you through the trial, and I saw the mistreatment. I will redeem it. I have your heart. I know you have chosen to walk with integrity to honor Me. You are My tablet, and I want to write your story for My glory and purposes. I've got you.*

The title of my first book was *Why Is My Raincoat "Dry Clean Only"? Obeying God's Instructions Even When They Don't Make Sense.* The publishing timeline was very tight. After months of writing, prayer, manuscript reviews from peers and friends, rewriting and editing, I submitted my manuscript to the publisher.

I eagerly checked my email, waiting for my editor's response. Being a first-time author, I knew my manuscript would need significant editing and polishing with the professionals. I was eager to learn and had emptied my calendar the following weeks to work alongside my editor toward the final manuscript.

Seven days after I had sent my manuscript, the email I had been anticipating arrived in my inbox. I opened the email with excitement, ready to start editing. The publisher's words came at me in agonizing slow motion. Tears stung my eyes, and my jaw dropped. I lost my breath and fell to the floor as shock and grief overwhelmed my heart. The editing process was not beginning; it wasn't even going to start. Here is just part of the email.

Sharon:

Have read your manuscript. In our opinion, this manuscript is not publishable. Several of us have reviewed it and while each of us found some things we liked about it, overall it is uneven and not cohesive.

So where does this leave us? As I said above, [publisher] has determined this is not a publishable manuscript … Therefore, pursuant to paragraph 8.4 of the publishing agreement we have elected to terminate the agreement in whole.

Not publishable. Not cohesive. Terminate the agreement in whole.

They didn't want my first book or my second.

Failure. Rejection. Humiliation.

I pulled myself up and wiped the carpet fibers off my face and called for my husband. Jim had encouraged me for many years to write and was delighted my books were being published. Hearing the pain in my voice, he hurried to me. He saw what was written all over my face. I was broken. Stunned. Humiliated. Still trying to catch my breath, I looked into his eyes, my voice and body both shaking. "They aren't going to publish my book." I showed him the email. He was equally stunned.

Why had God seemingly taken back this gift?

Failure. I failed to deliver a manuscript that the publisher would accept.

My world was rocked that day, but Christ's love and wisdom reflected through my children, Joshua and Gabrielle, picked me up and pointed me forward. "It's okay, Mom. You are not a failure. We love you. We are proud of you. The publisher is missing out on your books. That is their fail, not yours." The unconditional love and support from my husband and my children held me steady. The treasure of their grace gave me strength to deal with the fallout.

The two-book contract was indeed a gift from the Lord; it was just packaged differently than I originally thought. My failed and rejected manuscript made no sense at first. But God was protecting me. He was redirecting me. He was teaching me through my failure that living out the message of my book was far more important than having it published.

What can God do with our failures? He can redeem them. He can grow our measure of faith in Him. He can deepen our trust in Him. He can keep us humble and reliant on His power and provision. He can remind us that, even when things don't make sense, He is God and we are to honor and obey Him.

I believe my testimony is not over and that God will further redeem my failure. I am currently in that wilderness place tending to God's sheep, being refined and awaiting my burning-bush experience. I humbly look expectantly to God to use me through and despite my failures. I will labor as He leads because, otherwise, it will be in vain. "Unless the LORD builds the house, they labor in vain who build it; unless the LORD guards the city, the watchman stays awake in vain" (Ps. 127:1 NKJV).

God alone determines how He uses us through our failures, not man. He is sovereign. Like Moses, our assurance comes from knowing God is on the throne. He establishes peace for us. He accomplishes His purposes through us. "LORD, you establish peace for us; all that we have accomplished you have done for us. LORD our God, other lords besides you have ruled over us, but your name alone do we honor" (Isa. 26:12–13).

Chapter 3

What God Can Do through My Fears

Can I be faithful even though I'm afraid?

Fear: anything real or imagined that brings up thoughts of pain, suffering, loss, and doubt of God's love.

As a general rule, people are nosy, some more than others. We like to pull back the curtain and peek into the lives of others, to make comparisons, and dare I say, poke fun at their quirky idiosyncrasies. While people-peeking is fun to me, some real-life shows, in my opinion, go too far.

Reality TV shows began to multiply and reach a hungry audience in the early 2000s. My young son, who likes scary, gross, and daring, couldn't get enough of one such show that debuted in 2001 and has since influenced many talk shows and game shows and such with similar anxiety-laden challenges. But I would have nothing to do with this form of entertainment, appropriately titled *Fear Factor*. (If we were in the same room, I bet we would be fist-bumping about now.)

In *Fear Factor*, individuals, and sometimes teams, would dare to complete fearful and even gruesome tasks for the grand prize of $50,000 and to hear the words "evidently, fear is not a factor for you."[1] You may be thinking, *$50,000! I'd do just about anything for that kind of cash!* But would you? Really? There's not enough cash to entice me to jump from one building to another, hang on to the outside of a helicopter while flying over crocodile-infested water, eat vile parts of any animal, ingest insects, or walk on fire or broken glass. Nope. Not me. Not for any amount of money.

Through Christ, fear doesn't have to be a factor for us. However, and sadly, it often is a factor for us. Oh, that by the end of this chapter, our enemy would murmur under his breath, "Evidently, fear is no longer a factor for *her*." *(Please, Jesus, I pray it is so!)* It's possible! Do you believe it?

The apostle John wrote, "Such love has no fear, because perfect love expels all fear. If we are afraid, it is for fear of punishment, and this shows that we have not fully experienced his perfect love" (1 John 4:18 NLT). Can we marinate in this verse for a minute? How about underlining the phrase "perfect love expels all fear"? While immersing in the goodness of this truth, let's not trip over the word "perfect." We are not perfect, will not be made perfect, and will not perfectly love on this side of eternity. The perfect love John spoke of is the perfectly perfected or completely complete love that God has for His children. We can be so confident in His love for us, and in our judgment-free, secured future with Him, that all fear is expelled, cast out, and removed (choose your own synonym).

Perfect love expels all fear.

Because of His love we don't have to fear … but we do, and there's hope. The hope is found in verses prior. Would you underline "abides" in the passage below? (Your Bible might say "remain," "stay," or "live.")

> Whoever confesses that Jesus is the Son of God, God abides in him, and he in God. So we have come to know and to believe the love that God has for us. God is love, and whoever abides in love abides in God, and God abides in him. (1 John 4:15–16 ESV)

When we are saved, God lives in us. As we grow in our relationship with Him, we come to know and trust the security of His love. He continues to flourish in us. Picture the wild ivy that grows on a landscape border in a park. The ivy starts out small and almost unnoticeable, but little by little it grows thicker and fuller until one day the ivy consumes the wall completely. It's almost as if they have become one.

Abiding is a Bible word meaning "to be rooted in Him, knit to Him by the Spirit we have received from Him."[2] Like the ivy and the wall, our relationship with God will be as one. This love is perfect, and perfected in us by Him.

- We don't have to fear physical death: Jesus conquered it.
- We don't have to fear God's judgment: Jesus covered it.
- We don't have to fear eternal separation: Jesus closed it.
- We don't have to fear to live for God: Jesus confirms it.

My son has his own unique way of expressing his faith and belief in Jesus. Most people who believe in Jesus might say, "I'm a Christian" or "I'm a believer." He is a Christian, a believer in Jesus, but Griffin's Instagram bio says "Christian Raised." He's proud of the way he was raised, the Savior he lives for, and is not fearful to let others know. The love of God abides deeply in his nineteen-year-old frame.

Griffin is a heavy-equipment operator for a construction company. Recently, while at a stoplight on his lunch break, he noticed three homeless people sitting on a curb in a nearby parking lot. Like southerners do, he threw up his hand and waved. To his surprise, they smiled and waved back. The light turned green and he moved on. *Wow. They don't have anything, but they have joy.* His spirit quickened and gave instructions: turn back and give them the money in your wallet.

Now you have to understand, Griffin works hard, physically hard, for his money. He plans his spending well, so this rattled his cage. The sixty dollars was his weekly food allowance. His mind raced through all the reasons God's instructions didn't make sense.

He tried to problem-solve: *If I give them the money, then I guess I won't eat.* God continued to press his spirit to obey, so Griffin did.

He turned his truck around, drove into the parking lot, and walked right up to the ones the world has forgotten. Griffin exchanged some light banter; one wanted a hug so he hugged her, then he pulled out his wallet and handed them each a $20 bill, saying, "I'm buying your lunch today." All were very appreciative. Griffin responded using his bio tagline, "You're welcome. I'm Christian raised."

Abiding with God is the key to conquering fear.

God's perfect love cast out any fear Griffin had to obey the Spirit's directions. He didn't fear physical harm or financial provision. His love for, trust in, and respect for (reverential fear of) God threw out all human reasoning. He couldn't *not* obey.

Abiding with God is the key to conquering fear.

The bottom line is this: fear *should not* be a factor for us, but it is. We are humans and we are going to fear. Yes, you read correctly. We *are* going to fear. David, before he became Israel's king, wrote, "When I am afraid, I will put my trust in You" (Ps. 56:3 NASB). He penned these words regarding the time he was rejected by Achish, the Philistine king. Notice David didn't say *if* I fear. Fear will happen; we just can't allow it to steal our faith in the One whose perfect love was sacrificed to expel it.

When I Fear

For our study, let's define fear as anything real or imagined that brings up thoughts of pain, suffering, loss, and doubt of God's love.

Further, fear is anything we encounter that causes us to momentarily focus our thoughts on how we *feel* rather than on what we *know*. Fear not only directs our thoughts, but it also dictates our actions. This is why we need to learn to properly respond to fear.

Fear not only directs our thoughts, but it also dictates our actions.

My young adult daughter was home from college for Christmas break. We baked, worked puzzles, and watched old movies. I loved every single minute of her time at home, with the exception of one night.

She left our house to have lunch with a friend at 11:00 a.m. Fine. No issues. Have fun with your friend. All was good until midnight rolled around and there was no word from her. Texts were sporadically answered. Calls went to voice mail.

This *real* situation brought about imagined images of suffering. *What if her phone died and she's on the side of the road and someone stopped to help her and took her? The roads are wet, and she could've had a wreck. What if she is at the bottom of a ditch with a dead phone and a wrecked car?*

This *real* situation cultivated feelings of loss. *She's young. She hasn't finished college or had a family. Please, God, don't take her. Why would You take her now? You have good plans for her.*

I'm happy to report none of my imagined thoughts became reality. She was late, extremely late, but was safe. We had the obligatory mother-daughter, come-to-Jesus talk the next morning. She apologized. I forgave. All was right again.

In-the-moment fear is a normal part of life.

I had feared. Momentarily, I had let my thoughts run amok. As my girlfriend, you are probably sympathizing with me a bit. *You're a momma. You should have been concerned. This is normal. Don't beat yourself up.* All that's right and true. In-the-moment fear is a normal part of life. But when we allow fear to determine our actions, override our right thinking, and steal our general joy of living, then we have a problem.

In-the-moment fear is not a sin. Remember that David said "when I fear," not *if* I fear. In the next part of that verse, David gave the antidote to fear: trust. Trust is believing God can and will, even if He hasn't yet. Fear becomes a sin when in-the-moment turns into a way of life. Fear becomes sin when it shouts louder than our faith and God's truth is no longer our source of wisdom, guidance, knowledge, and peace. The imagined overcomes the real; unbelief silences belief.

Fear becomes a sin when in-the-moment turns into a way of life.

Fear is one of the greatest tools the enemy has in his armory to use against us. If he can cause us to doubt God and God's Word, he wins. The writer of Proverbs called fear a snare or trap. "The fear of man lays a snare, but whoever trusts in the LORD is safe" (Prov. 29:25 ESV). Maybe you can relate to the following:

- You experience a pain in the same place so-and-so experienced pain. She passed away from cancer. Your great aunt on your momma's cousin's side of the family had a similar problem. She also passed away at a young age. Before you even schedule a visit to the doctor, fear has diagnosed you with a disease and put you in the grave.

- You text and call your really good friend. Several days go by without a response. You try again. Still no response. You've never been able to maintain a close friendship, so you fear she's dumped you like all the others. Then you see her at the Mexican restaurant with some other girls. Instead of saying something, you allow fear to make you assume she no longer wants to be your friend. You stop liking her social media posts and sitting near her in church.

- You have a dream that you will be a young widow, left to raise your children alone. Every time your husband gets on a plane, you fear his plane will crash. While he is away, you are edgy and don't sleep. Your mind is consumed with "what if" scenarios of how you will manage without him. If he doesn't respond quickly to your messages, you assume something has happened to him. Fear has stolen peace and sleep, not to mention precious time with your children while your husband was away.

Fear is a thief that steals our peaceful living, our confidence in the love of the One who made us, and it meddles in our rational thinking, causing us to doubt everything we know about God.

God knows fear is going to be part of our lives. The Bible speaks of fear over three hundred times. In fact, in a quick search of the phrase "do not be afraid," God told Moses and Joshua not to be afraid in thirteen different references. What amazes me is neither of these men told God they were afraid. God *knew* they were afraid. God knows when you are afraid. We will learn through the life of Moses that God doesn't count our fear against us. He helps us work through it, then uses it for His glory and our good. All this being true, where do we go from here? What is our proper response to fear?

God doesn't count our fear against us.

We have to overpower in-the-moment fear so that it doesn't become way-of-life fear. I know, this sounds good when I say it, and it looks doable in print. This is only possible when we allow our lives to intersect with God's Word to change our thinking and build a trust relationship with God. In order to get a hold of our fear, we have to allow the Spirit to get a hold on us.

May I pause to interject a disclaimer before I move on? I like to shoot straight with my friends. I am not a licensed counselor, and I'm not pretending to be. What I am about to prescribe is biblical, not psychological. I have very dear people in my life who deal with way-of-life fear and at times are paralyzed by it. I take it very seriously. If you struggle with constant, persistent fear and anxiety that are making it hard for you to live your life, please seek professional Christian counseling in addition to the simple prescription I am about to share. Christian counselors join the psychological and physiological with biblical truths. I believe in counseling, and I love the people who have committed their lives to helping others live victoriously.

Now that we've had our public-service announcement, let's get back to work. If we want to have a proper response to fear, we have to take steps to develop fear's antidote—trust.

1. Pause. Recognize fear in the moment. Fear is creeping in when our thoughts move from rational to irrational, our spirit becomes anxious, even our breathing can become ramped up, and we can experience confusion. When the panic starts to happen, pause.

2. Pray out loud in the pause. The enemy can't hear your silent prayers (you're not talking to him!), so pray out loud! In your prayer admit that you are afraid, that you don't understand what is happening, and ask God for His peace. Tell God you trust Him and are confident that He will work things out for your good.

3. Put off making major decisions during in-the-moment fear.

4. Put it in writing. Make a note of the event as soon as you can. Write down what you were doing and your physical and psychological response. Having notes will help you remember so you can recognize a pattern.

5. Probe. Use a Bible-commentary site or resource to research scriptures having to do with fear and peace. Write these scriptures on note cards. Read these scriptures out loud on a daily basis. Keep this mini Bible of truths with you so *when* you fear, you can put your trust in God and His Word. Having the mini Bible is especially helpful because in the moment it is difficult to recall scriptures from memory.

The fear factor has two sides. There is the fear that comes from the father of lies, who is Satan (John 8:44). He longs to trap us in fear and anxiety and separate us from reality and from God. The flip side of that is the holy fear of our heavenly Father, which sets us free (John 8:31–32) and is the beginning of wisdom. Did you notice one fear seeks to trap, while the other sets us free? In this next section we'll talk about being free.

The Fear That Frees

The fear that frees is the reverential awe or deep respect for God. This fear recognizes God's power and creates an overwhelming desire to submit to His greatness in the heart of the believer. Martin Luther, the leader of the Protestant Reformation, painted a far more beautiful picture of fear that frees than I could ever write.

He distinguished between what he called a *servile* fear and a *filial* fear.

> The servile fear is a kind of fear that a prisoner in a torture chamber has for his tormentor, the jailer, or the executioner. It's that kind of dreadful anxiety in which someone is frightened by the clear and present danger that is represented by another person. Or it's the kind of fear that a slave would have at the hands of a malicious master who would come with the whip and torment the slave. Servile refers to a posture of servitude toward a malevolent owner.
>
> Luther distinguished between that and what he called filial fear, drawing from the Latin concept from which we get the idea of family. It refers to the fear that a child has for his father. In this regard, Luther is thinking of a child who has tremendous respect and love for his father or mother and who dearly wants to please them. He has a fear or an anxiety of offending the one he loves, not because he's afraid

of torture or even of punishment, but rather because he's afraid of displeasing the one who is, in that child's world, the source of security and love.[3]

In the Old Testament, God's people were told never to forget the holiness and power of God—even speaking the name of God was taken very seriously. They had seen with their own eyes, or heard testimony of, His power demonstrated in the flood, plagues, parting of the sea, and military victories of the One True God, and dared not risk offending Him by misrepresenting His name. There was so much respect and reverence for His name that substitutions were created. Adonai or Hashem was used in place of His name. In fact, the Hebrew name for God, made up of four consonants (YHWH), was spoken only once a year at Yom Kippur (the Day of Atonement, the holiest day of the year in Judaism) by the high priest. In our study, we have identified the names of God. Can you imagine not ever uttering them?

God is a God who loves to bless His children with love, mercy, and grace, but He is also a God of justice, discipline, and wrath.

In the New Testament, we are invited to call God the personal name of Abba, which means "Father" or "Daddy." We are invited to boldly approach His throne (Heb. 4:15–16) because He understands and empathizes with our weaknesses. Oh, let's not forget that Abba of the New Testament is also Hashem of the Old Testament. The same God who cleared out the enemies for the tribes of Israel in order for them to move into the Promised Land also raised the dead to life, gave sight to the blind, healed the lame, and made the sick well. Oh, that we never forget when we approach the throne to talk to our Daddy, that He is the one who created the world with His words and destroyed it with a flood.

God is a God who loves to bless His children with love, mercy, and grace, but He is also a God of justice, discipline, and wrath. When we get caught up in the former and forget the latter, we have an improper and, might I say, a disrespectful view of fear of the Lord.

- He will display love but will serve justice.
- He will offer mercy but will send discipline.
- He will extend grace but will serve wrath.

This Hashem, this Adonai, is the God Moses knew of—the One he revered. Imagine his surprise when this One, whose name no one would speak, spoke to him. In a moment, God called Moses to the assignment of a lifetime, caused him to confront his fears, and confirmed that his fear had not disqualified him from serving.

Moses's Moment

In the last chapter, we left Moses kneeling by a talking burning bush. The voice speaking we now know was Hashem, God Himself. Let's refresh our minds with the scripture's account of the moment.

> There the angel of the LORD appeared to him in flames of fire from within a bush. Moses saw that though the bush was on fire it did not burn up. So Moses thought, "I will

go over and see this strange sight—why the bush does not burn up."

When the LORD saw that he had gone over to look, God called to him from within the bush, "Moses! Moses!"

And Moses said, "Here I am." (Ex. 3:2–4)

Moses was eighty years young when God called him for the assignment of a lifetime. He was no longer a young, well-respected Egyptian, and likely not as strong as he once was. The fine things of palace life had passed him by. The pushing down and repressing of what he had done no doubt had taken a toll on his mind, body, soul, and spirit. A man of eighty years, and he had nothing to show for himself. He tended sheep that didn't even belong to him, an occupation despised by the Egyptians: "When he does, be sure to say, 'We are shepherds. Our families have always raised sheep.' If you tell him this, he will let you settle in the region of Goshen. Joseph wanted them to say this to the king, because the Egyptians did not like to be around anyone who raised sheep" (Gen. 46:34 CEV).

My, how far Moses had fallen.

This old man of broken spirit and low esteem moved his flock to the far side of the desert to an area near Horeb, also known as Sinai or the mountain of God. Horeb had fertile valleys and water was plentiful. All shepherds drove their flocks to this area because of its abundance. So, on a day when Moses was doing what was expected, something very unexpected happened. What a lesson we can learn in this moment: leave room for the unexpected; this is when we see God show off.

Leave room for the unexpected; this is when we see God show off.

The desert separated Horeb from Midian, where Moses lived with his family and father-in-law. While crossing the land on the way to the rich ground of Horeb, he saw a burning bush. In the extreme dry desert plains, it was not unusual for a bush to spontaneously burst into flames; however, it was quite peculiar for the fire not to consume the bush and for the bush to speak.

With caution and curiosity, Moses approached this phenomenon. I absolutely love his first response: he talked to himself. "So Moses thought, 'I will go over and see this strange sight—why the bush does not burn up'" (Ex. 3:3). This allows us to experience the human side of Moses in a moment of fear. I mean, haven't we all had one-on-one conversations with ourselves? Then Moses's moment grew more intense and fearful. A voice from the bush spoke, and not only did it speak, but the voice knew Moses's name. I can only imagine what Moses might have been saying to himself at this point.

With sweaty palms and a rapid heartbeat, perhaps these thoughts raced through his mind: *God knows. He knows my name, what I did, and where I am. Now I must answer for my actions in Egypt. My past has finally caught up with me.*

Much to his surprise, though, this was a voice of calling, not condemnation; restoration, not ruin; and deliverance, not death. In the moment of fear, God spoke, revealing Himself to Moses.

When the LORD saw that he had gone over to look, God called to him from within the bush, "Moses! Moses!"

And Moses said, "Here I am." (Ex. 3:4)

An appearance of God in the Bible (often in human form, but not always) that can be seen or heard or physically experienced is called a theophany.[4] This type of encounter occurred with other individuals: Abraham (Gen. 12:7–9; 18:1–33), Jacob (Gen. 32:22–30), and Job (Job 38–42). We can find theophanies on a greater scale in the pillar of cloud and fire by night that directed the Israelites in the desert after the exodus from Egypt. There's no doubt, God makes himself known to His children.

This first exchange between Moses and God was special. When God called Moses's name, Moses didn't answer, "Who is it?" Moses knew who was speaking to him. Maybe you are a wonderer like me. I'm curious and always have been. I wondered how Moses knew it was God speaking to him. Had they enjoyed morning walks together and quiet times under the stars? Scripture doesn't record any dialogue between Moses and God when he fled Egypt to Midian. So how did he know?

The apostle Paul has a wonderful response for all the wonderers, "For since the creation of the world God's invisible qualities—his eternal power and divine nature—have been clearly seen, being understood from what has been made, so that people are without excuse" (Rom. 1:20). When God reaches out to reveal Himself to His children, they know without a doubt that it is God, especially when He speaks from a bush. Do you recall when God first revealed Himself to you? As we mature in our faith and seek Him, let's pray for more and more revelation from God, from burning bushes, beautiful orange sunsets, solid biblical teaching, or soft whispers to our heart.

Do you recall when God first revealed Himself to you?

God called Moses twice. This too is fascinating and not the first time God called a person for an assignment of a lifetime and shouted his name twice.

- "Abraham! Abraham!" (Gen. 22:11)—God called Abraham to sacrifice Isaac.
- "Jacob! Jacob!" (Gen. 46:2)—God called Jacob to move his family to Egypt.
- "Samuel! Samuel!" (1 Sam. 3:10)—God called to Samuel about the judgment of Eli.

God revealed Himself to each person in a moment. Moses had the same response as all the men listed above, "Here I am." Even more, Moses obeyed God. He removed his shoes, hid his face, and bowed his knee. His actions demonstrated reverential, respectful fear—the right fear—before the holy God, Elohim the infinite, all-powerful God who is the creator, sustainer, and judge of the world. Wow!

God told Moses exactly who was speaking to him, "The LORD said, 'I have indeed seen the misery of my people in Egypt. I have heard them crying out because of their slave drivers, and I am concerned about their suffering'" (Ex. 3:7). And then God belted out Moses's assignment:

And now the cry of the Israelites has reached me, and I have seen the way the Egyptians are oppressing them. So now, go. I am sending you to Pharaoh to bring my people the Israelites out of Egypt. (Ex. 3:9–10)

With these words hanging in the air, "I am sending you," Moses began to confront his fears. In a single moment he was being promoted from lowly shepherd to the deliverer of God's people, his people.

Moses Confronts His Fear

As if kneeling on holy ground before Elohim wasn't overwhelming enough, Moses heard the calling God placed on his life. It's natural to consider that in this moment his right fear immediately shifted gears. When we read the scriptures that begin with "Moses said to God" in Exodus chapters 3 and 4, we can hear Moses's fear and anxiety. He told God, "Here I am," but the reality of what was happening had to be sinking in. Like most of us when we are called to assignment, Moses had lots of questions and worries.

- "Who am I that I should go to Pharaoh and bring the Israelites out of Egypt?" (Ex. 3:11).
- "Suppose I go to the Israelites and say to them, 'The God of your fathers has sent me to you,' and they ask me, 'What is his name?' Then what shall I tell them?" (Ex. 3:13).
- "Pardon your servant, Lord. I have never been eloquent, neither in the past nor since you have spoken to your servant. I am slow of speech and tongue" (Ex. 4:10).

- "But Moses said, 'Pardon your servant, Lord. Please send someone else'" (Ex. 4:13).

We can assume Moses was still barefoot and bowed down before the burning bush at this point. I wonder if his mind flashed back to the time when his attempt to rescue his people resulted in murder and his cowardly flight to Midian. Maybe he was thinking about how he had spent years mostly walking in the dust and talking to sheep, and now God wanted him to make a demand of a king? Seriously? Moses was human—all these thoughts and more had to be racing through his mind.

Did he …

- fear going back to the scene of the crime?
- fear they would remember?
- fear his own people would reject him?
- fear he wasn't qualified?

The wrong fear is prone to creep in when we shift our focus away from God and onto our abilities, strengths, and qualifications. When our gaze is fixed on the assignment, rather than on the One who assigns, we are likely to fear and possibly bolt. Elohim, the creator God, the One who is supreme over all things, the One who spoke to Moses, is our God. We can be confident that when He calls us to an assignment, He will complete the assignment, using our fears and anxiety as powerful tools in the process.

Being afraid is natural.

Being afraid is natural. God longs to help us face our in-the-moment fear so that it doesn't become way-of-life fear and keep us from enjoying all that He has planned for us.

Even though God was speaking directly to him, and he believed God to be the maker of the universe, Moses still had moments of fear:

- The LORD said to Moses, "Do not be afraid."

As the Israelites progressed to the Promised Land, they encountered hostile territories. After defeating the Ammonites, Moses and the people faced King Og of Bashan (Num. 21:34).

- The LORD said to me, "Do not be afraid."

God repeated to Moses His "do not be afraid" message as Moses approached King Og (Deut. 3:2).

Moses kept his gaze on God, and God continued to be patient with Moses, using him in the great story of deliverance. Our God is greater than our fear and longs to walk with us triumphantly, fear-free. The Lord is our Helper, and we don't have to be afraid (Heb. 13:6). No weapon forged against us will prevail (Isa. 54:17). Write these two truths in your mini Bible for future use.

Fear Is Not a Disqualifier

In that moment, God called Moses to his assignment, caused him to face his fear, and confirmed that fear was not a disqualifier. If fear were a disqualifier for serving God, then God wouldn't have chosen ...

- Elijah to face down King Ahab and his meddling wife, Jezebel.
- Esther to address King Ahasuerus to save the Jewish people.
- Saul to be the king of Israel.
- Peter to feed His sheep.

Fear is not a disqualifier; it's an invitation.

And Moses would not have been chosen to be the deliverer of God's people. The fear he displayed when he ran from Egypt after killing the soldier would have surely been enough to cancel any plans God had for him, but that is not how God handles our weaknesses. God forgives and restores. He is the lifter of our head, and the author of our story.

I have no doubt God used the forty years between Egypt and Horeb to humble Moses. He learned the best leaders are servants, authority is to be respected, and the finer things of the world aren't all that important. Fear may drive us from God for a season, but never so far that His arm can't reach us.

Oh, the pages that have been filled with words of wisdom on the subject of fear! I don't dare to even guess how many books concerning fear there are, written by authors I deeply respect. In this chapter I want us to walk away with simple truths tucked in our heart and mind for safe keeping until we find ourselves in a moment of fear.

1. Fear is not an excuse to disobey God.
2. Fear is not a sin, unless or until it causes us to doubt God and separates us from His truth.

3. Fear is not a disqualifier for God's work; it's an invitation.

It is possible to be faithful and fearful at the same time.

Max Lucado is one of the incredibly gifted authors who I referenced in the previous paragraph. I choose to close this chapter with his wise words: "The presence of fear does not mean you have no faith. Fear visits everyone. But make your fear a visitor, not a resident."[5] It is possible to be faithful and fearful at the same time.

Reflecting on What God Can Do with My Fear

1. Fear *should not* be a factor for us, but it is. Fear gives us the opportunity to trust God. David, Israel's greatest king, mightiest warrior, and killer of Goliath, feared. He wrote, "When I am afraid, I will put my trust in You" (Ps. 56:3 NASB). In what do you trust? Who do you turn to when you are afraid?

2. Fear is anything we encounter that causes us to momentarily adjust our thoughts from what we *know* to how we *feel*. Moses felt fear after he murdered the Egyptian and ran. He felt fear as he heard God's

plan for his life. How has fear directed your actions and emotions when it comes to faithfully following God?

3. My greatest fear is living out my days without my husband. At times it has paralyzed me, taking a physiological toll. In those moments I have to verbally tell myself what I *know* so what I *feel* will flee. Will you trust God with your greatest fear? Tell Him so in a simple prayer as you picture yourself casting your cares on Him (1 Pet. 5:7).

4. Wrestle with these statements about fear. Which do you struggle with the most, and why?

- Fear is not an excuse to disobey God.
- Fear is not a sin, unless or until it causes us to doubt God and separate us from His truth.

- Fear is not a disqualifier for God's work; it's an invitation.

5. We discussed a right fear in this chapter. "The fear of man lays a snare, but whoever trusts in the LORD is safe" (Prov. 29:25 ESV). This fear is not an "I am scared" fear. Fear in this sense means to respect and revere God. What are ways you show God respect?

Revealing My Potential

Use the space provided to respond to this prompt: What has God revealed to you about fear? What has He shown you about your particular fears?

_____

_____

_____

_____

_____

_____

_____

_____

_____

_____

Possibility Profile: Sherri

I was married to my husband, Harry, for twenty-eight years. Happily married. We had a good life. We had three daughters that we adored; he had a successful business; we were involved in our church, community, and our girls' schools. We were comfortable. And happy. Although there were things I was afraid of, I never feared losing him. At least not when I was forty-eight.

On August 18, 2013, he took his life. I had no warning, no suspicions, no preparation. The word *fear* took on a whole new meaning for me.

I was left to finish raising three daughters. Alone. He was the breadwinner, the financial supporter of our family. I now had to take that responsibility on. I had never even paid a bill. So many new fears that I had never even considered flooded my mind. I was devastated. Heartbroken. Afraid.

I've known about Jesus all my life. I accepted Him at the age of ten. I had always believed in Him and believed Him. I had always trusted Him. I had had difficult circumstances and continued to trust Him. Could I do it *now*? Could I continue to trust Him when I was so afraid of the future without my husband?

Since I had grown up believing God and trusting Him, it was actually very natural for me to trust Him during my worst nightmare. The very night Harry died, as soon as I lay down in bed between two devastated, scared girls, Psalm 56:3 popped into my mind. The Lord was saying to me, "I know this is scary. I know you're afraid. You can still trust Me!" Another scripture that came to mind that night was Hebrews 13:8, which says, "Jesus Christ is the same yesterday, today, yes and forever." I realized on my worst day that Jesus hadn't changed and that I could indeed trust Him even through this.

Although I had so many questions and did not understand why God had allowed this at all, I was never angry with Him. I know nothing happens without His permission. Though I couldn't imagine why He had allowed this, I trusted Him and His plan.

After Harry died, I began to learn about some things he was involved in that were unethical and illegal. I found myself in the middle of lawsuits because of activity I knew nothing about. New fears abounded again. About two years after he died, I was diagnosed with breast cancer. More fears. I would get past one fear, and another would take its place. That's how it happens in life!

Here are some things I've learned over the last five and a half years: God is a faithful God. Always. Even when our situations are horrible and we don't understand, and we're afraid, He's still the same God He was during the twenty-eight years I was happily married to my husband. Sometimes I don't *feel* like He's present. Sometimes I don't *feel* like He's taking care of me. But I've learned that I can't count on what I feel. Feelings are liars. I have to lean on the things I KNOW, not what I FEEL. I *know* He's always with me (Matt. 28:20; Josh. 1:9). I *know* He takes care of me (1 Pet. 5:7). I can't count on feelings, but I can count on the truth in God's Word every single time!

God will walk with us through our fears and get us through our most difficult times. In John 16:33, He tells us we will have trouble, but He promises to be with us in that trouble. According to Isaiah 43:2, He will protect us when we face difficult circumstances.

Another thing God has shown me over and over is that He is our one sure thing, our real security. We can't put our faith and trust in anyone or anything else. Those things will disappoint us and let us down. We try to find our security and fulfillment in people and things, but it never works. I felt secure when I was married to Harry, but he left me. Isaiah 26:4 tells me to trust in God forever, that He is an everlasting rock! Even the best people let us down! God will never let us down. Never.

I'm approaching six years without Harry. There have been many times I've been afraid. I still feel afraid of lots of things. I don't always get the trust thing right. But God, my sweet Father, gently pulls me back into the truth: when I am afraid, I can trust in Him. I know Him so much differently than I did six years ago. I trust Him so much more than I did six years ago. I can share Him differently than I could six years ago. I love Him more and more deeply than I did six years ago. Second Corinthians 1:3–4 reminds me that God is the God of all comfort. He has comforted me during my struggle so that I can share that comfort with others who are struggling. He has given me so many opportunities to comfort other young widows and assure them that He is faithful.

I have seen God protect my family and provide for us in ways I could never have imagined. He has comforted me and given me strength in ways that I could never explain or understand. I've always known Him, but I really know Him now. I feel like Job—now my eyes have seen Him (Job 42:5). I know the only way we have kept going is because of His faithfulness.

Here are some things that have helped me: digging into God's Word, focusing on Him and not my circumstances, having a thankful attitude, and replacing my negative thoughts with truth from His Word. There is nothing more helpful to us during our everyday lives and during crises than God's Word. It truly has everything we need in it: comfort, encouragement, guidance, direction, instruction.

One of the main ways I've gotten through my fears is to focus on Him and not the fear. My favorite scripture is Isaiah 26:3. It promises that I will have perfect peace if I "stay my mind" on Him. Peace is the opposite of fear. I want peace! So, I try to keep my focus on Jesus. One way I do that is by thanking Him for the gifts He has given me. When I'm thankful, I am thankful to the Giver, and He's the Giver of all good gifts (James 1:17).

When I do begin to focus on my fears or my scary circumstances, I have to remember not to trust my feelings. I go to the Bible and find scripture to combat the lies I'm starting to believe. When I'm afraid, I go to verses like Zephaniah 3:17. That tells me He will calm all my fears with His love. It also tells me He rejoices over me and delights in me. Wow! He will take care of my fears, and He thinks I'm delightful!

Life is scary. There will always be things we will be afraid of. Because I knew the Lord and trusted Him, I was able to move forward and not let my fear paralyze me. My best advice for facing fear is this: Focus on Jesus. Now. Before the fear hits. Get to know Him. Get to know everything about Him you possibly can. Spend time in His Word. Get closer to Him. Then, when scary times come or the unimaginable happens, it will be completely natural for you to lean on Him. And He will always deliver! He never disappoints.

Chapter 4

What God Can Do through My Frailties

Am I valuable even though I feel damaged?

*Frailty: something we didn't and don't
have control over but can still be used
for our good and God's glory.*

Have you ever heard the saying "Be careful what you pray for"? Joni accepted Jesus as her Savior when she was fourteen years old. However, in the years following her decision, she fell short of living as Christ would have her live. As she prepared to graduate from high school and leave for college, she longed for things to be different. She prayed a very brave and simple prayer that would change her life forever.

> Lord, I'm not doing this thing called Christian right, and I know it. I don't want to go off to college and defame your good name or smear your reputation. I know it's about far more than just me, so do something in my life to jerk it right side up, because I'm really living this life wrong.[1]

Later that summer, Joni's sister asked her to go to the beach for a swim. Joni accepted the invitation. When she arrived at the beach, she swam right out to a floating raft. Joni was very athletic and swam the distance without stopping or touching the bottom. She quickly climbed up on the raft and dove into extremely shallow water. She hit the lake floor headfirst, snapping her neck and crushing her fourth cervical vertebra. The break immediately severed her spinal cord.

In the same moment, standing on the shoreline with her back turned from the raft, Joni's sister was startled when a crab bit her toe. As she turned to warn Joni of the hungry crabs, Kathy saw her sister's blond hair floating on the surface of the water. She franticly swam out to save her sister. But what had she saved Joni for? Life as a paraplegic? A life sitting down, unable to do anything for herself? What kind of life would that be? Later in the hospital, Joni thought, "*God, is this Your idea of an answer to my prayer to be drawn closer to*

You? If it is, You are never going to be trusted with another one of my prayers again. I mean, I'm a new Christian, how could You have taken me so seriously?"[2]

Despite the love and encouragement from her family and good Christian friends, during her rehabilitation Joni doubted God, had thoughts of suicide, and sank into a deep depression.

Joni desperately wanted to live for Christ. She poured out her heart to Him, and what did she get? In her opinion, a prayer answered wrong. She was damaged. She wondered how she could be of value to God or anyone else confined to a wheelchair, unable to use her arms or legs.

As part of her recovery process, Joni went to occupational therapy (OT) to learn ways to adapt and function in her new life. It was in OT that Joni learned to paint, not with her hands, but with her mouth—yes, her mouth. Little by little she was lifted out of the muck and mire of her depressed state, and Joni began to understand that God had used her unwise decision to answer her prayer.

Joni Eareckson Tada continues to paint, sing, and through voice recognition has become a bestselling author, writing more than fifty books. In 1979, she founded Joni and Friends, an organization designated to advancing Christian ministry in the disability community. Joni and Friends opened its International Disability Center in 2007. God did answer Joni's prayer. He jerked her life right side up and helped her live the Christian life in reverential fear.

It's so easy to look at our circumstances—lack of education, limited resources, low esteem, or lessened physical abilities—and wonder, *Am I valuable even though I feel damaged?* When Joni took her eyes off her *lack*, she was able to embrace her *lot*. Our lacks don't matter to God. When we are willing to walk in faith and right fear, God works in us and through us in spite of what we lack. The truth is, we all have a lot to offer God. Our lot has nothing to do with education, money, or ability. God doesn't look at our abilities; He looks at our availability.

Our lacks don't matter to God.

After his conversation with God, Moses had a lack that felt like a weighted cloak. His gaze was fixed on his call, and his mind raced to determine how someone like him could complete all that God expected. Isn't this true of me and you? We have a desire to serve God, maybe we even see an opportunity to serve, but we look at our lack, tuck our head into our slouched shoulders, and decide we don't have what it takes.

Israel's deliverer did the same thing. Kneeling on the dusty desert floor, Moses avowed to Elohim all his lack. I can't begin to imagine what God, who is acquainted with our ways, who fearfully and wonderfully created us in our mothers' wombs, and whose thoughts are precious toward us (Ps. 139:3, 14, 17), thinks when we declare our lack to Him. Such proclamations must grieve His heart. I'm so thankful God doesn't hold my senseless, fearful utterances against me, aren't you?

Through his utterances we can hear Moses list his frailties.

- "Who am I that I should go to Pharaoh and bring
  the Israelites out of Egypt?" (Ex. 3:11).
  Translated frailty: I'm lowly, a nobody. I have no
  power or position.

- "Suppose I go to the Israelites and say to them, 'The God of your fathers has sent me to you,' and they ask me, 'What is his name?' Then what shall I tell them?" (Ex. 3:13).
Translated frailty: I'm not smart or trusted. I have no authority.

- "Pardon your servant, Lord. I have never been eloquent, neither in the past nor since you have spoken to your servant. I am slow of speech and tongue" (Ex. 4:10).
Translated frailty: I'm not a good communicator.

- "But Moses said, 'Pardon your servant, Lord. Please send someone else.'" (Ex. 4:13).
Translated frailty: I'm not at all qualified or confident enough for this assignment.

Moses got on board with God's plan but not before a lengthy dialogue with Him. Moses stood on his shaky trust while God repaired his fractured faith and revealed his hidden potential. Moses's story gives all of us hope as we look at our lack. Moses eventually developed strong leader legs and completed the assignment in defiance of his frailties.

How did Moses walk out his calling with his frailties? The market is saturated with books encouraging us to find our strengths, to expand our strengths, and to live in our strengths. Workshops. Podcasts. Seminars. Retreats. Just do a Google search for "develop strength" and your options seem limitless. Moses had Elohim to help with his frailties. His Resource was and is limitless. And better yet, his Resource was never wrong.

God specializes in seeing the possible in people.

God specializes in seeing the possible in people. He chose Saul, who was from the tribe of Benjamin, the smallest of all the twelve tribes of Jacob, to become king of Israel. Ruth was a distrusted foreigner and a penniless widow who committed to stay with her also widowed mother-in-law, Naomi. Ruth, a non-Jew, later married Boaz, had a baby, and became part of the lineage of Jesus, king of the Jews. And there's Moses, a stuttering shepherd and fugitive, chosen to rescue God's people from the bondage of Egyptian slavery.

God sees the possible in you, and believes you are worthwhile. He sent His Son to die so you could live life full and free for eternity. The wonderer in me is asking, *Why would a God who sent His Son so I could live full and free saddle me with a frailty?* Perhaps you have asked the same question or one similar: Why can't I get ahead financially? Why was I born without sight? Why have I lost my hearing when I am only twenty? Why can't I afford to go to college and improve my skills? Why do I have this chronic illness? Why do I have to suffer depression and anxiety? Why? Why? Why?

God sees the possible in you, and believes you are worthwhile.

My friend, as I type these words, tears fill my eyes. Oh, how I would love to sit across from you, take your hand in mine, and answer your why. All I know is what I know … God loves you and has purposed every event in your life. His plan for you is good, and His definition of good is better than ours, even though we don't understand it. I know this because I've read His Word and I've witnessed for myself one life after another who thought their frailty made them worthless to God, yet victoriously lived to testify of God's power and glory. He wouldn't do this for others and not for you. While I can't answer why, I can say with confidence:

> But God chose what is foolish in the world to shame the wise; God chose what is weak in the world to shame the strong. (1 Cor. 1:27 ESV)

> But he said to me, "My grace is sufficient for you, for my power is made perfect in weakness." Therefore I will boast all the more gladly of my weaknesses, so that the power of Christ may rest upon me. (2 Cor. 12:9 ESV)

> "Neither this man nor his parents sinned," said Jesus, "but this happened so that the works of God might be displayed in him." (John 9:3)

In the remaining part of the chapter we are going to address each of Moses's fearful questions about his weakest attributes and find scriptural truth to build our confidence to steady our shaky, fractured faith. Shaky trust is better than no trust.

Shaky trust is better than no trust.

Frailty: Lack of Self-Worth

Failure and fear sure can feed the frailty of self-worth. Our world tells us worth comes from, or at the very least is associated with, position, power, possessions, and prestige. If we have a six-figure job, the wherewithal to accomplish important tasks, a fine home, high-end cars, and personal influence, then we will have value. If this were true, then why are the wealthiest, most well-known, and most well-educated people in America often the most unhappy, troubled, and heavyhearted? When our source for self-worth is self-accomplishment and self-recognition, we will always fall short in our own eyes.

Our self-worth is found in understanding and believing that our value comes through Christ. The understanding comes from our study of what the Scriptures say about us, but the believing comes from deep in the hidden places of our heart and mind. In those deep places we can silence the lying whispers with the Truth:

- *You came from the wrong side of the road.* It doesn't matter where I came from that matters; it's where I am going that counts.
- *Your record is failure.* It doesn't matter what I accomplished, or didn't accomplish; it's what I'm doing now that counts.
- *You're just like your alcoholic daddy.* The look I'm going for is to resemble my heavenly Father, and I'm looking more like Him every day.

We believe what we know.

We believe what we know. When we know the truth about our value to God, we will believe we are valuable regardless of what lies the evil one and voices of the world try to tell us. This is what your heavenly Daddy says:

- You are loved and whole: "Therefore, as God's chosen people, holy and dearly loved, clothe yourselves with compassion, kindness, humility, gentleness and patience" (Col. 3:12).

- You are justified and redeemed: "And all are justified freely by his grace through the redemption that came by Christ Jesus" (Rom. 3:24).

- You are no longer a slave to sin: "For we know that our old self was crucified with him so that the body ruled by sin might be done away with, that we should no longer be slaves to sin" (Rom. 6:6).

- You are not condemned: "Therefore, there is now no condemnation for those who are in Christ Jesus" (Rom. 8:1).

- You are an heir with Christ: "Now if we are children, then we are heirs—heirs of God and co-heirs with Christ, if indeed we share in his sufferings in order that we may also share in his glory" (Rom. 8:17).

You might need two mini Bibles by the end of this book. Praise God that His truth has the power to set us free by reminding us of who we are! Believe these truths, dear one. This is how your Daddy feels about you. These are the thoughts He has concerning you. Your worth is defined by what He says, not what the world says. Since Moses didn't have the New Testament for heart encouragement, God acknowledged each of Moses's frailties, including his lack of self-worth.

Your worth is defined by what God says, not what the world says.

Who am I that I should go to Pharaoh and bring the Israelites out of Egypt? (Ex. 3:11)

And God said, "I will be with you. And this will be the sign to you that it is I who have sent you: When you have brought the people out of Egypt, you will worship God on this mountain." (Ex. 3:12)

Oh, please, pretty please, underline the word "when." Did you hear God's love for Moses? *I hear your concern. Pharaoh is powerful and you don't feel worthy, but don't worry about anything. I'm going to be with you the entire time. You and I will meet right back here. You will worship Me here.* One would think these words would be enough to make Moses say, "I'm all in! Let's do this." However, our shepherd wasn't quite ready to accept his new title.

Frailty: Lack of Education

We can assume that Moses was educated because he was raised as part of the royal family. Records indicate Egypt had a great university. Naturally, the son of Pharaoh's daughter would have had the finest of everything. He most likely studied astronomy, mathematics, music, art, and of course, reading and writing.

Moses was schooled, and he was also trained. He lived in Pharaoh's house, dined with Pharaoh's people, and most importantly, was raised by Pharaoh's daughter. Not all education happens in a classroom. God used Moses's experience in the palace to train him for his future assignment. What about you? Can you trace the finger of God to a time that seemed unnatural or out of place for you? Perhaps, like God placing a Hebrew in the enemy camp, God is training you or has trained you for an assignment you think you aren't prepared to accept.

So, if Moses had all this education and experience, why did he ask an additional question about his new position? I believe he asked because he anticipated a forthcoming question from the Hebrews, a question that was not just about knowledge that comes through formal education, but knowledge that comes through lived experience. And Moses realized he did not have that experience with the Hebrews, even though he was one of them—he did not have the authenticity and authority of one who had lived among the slaves and learned their history. Though he had an education, he didn't have the right education.

> Suppose I go to the Israelites and say to them, "The God of your fathers has sent me to you," and they ask me, "What is his name?" Then what shall I tell them? (Ex. 3:13)

Moses had been introduced, quite dramatically I might add, to Elohim, but he realized he didn't have enough information about God to confidently convince the others to trust him as their deliverer. I believe he realized a weak part that needed strengthening, and God gave him a crash course.

> God said to Moses, "I AM WHO I AM. This is what you are to say to the Israelites: 'I AM has sent me to you.'"
> God also said to Moses, "Say to the Israelites, 'The LORD, the God of your fathers—the God of Abraham, the God of Isaac and the God of Jacob—has sent me to you.'" (Ex. 3:14–15)

After reading this response, maybe you're feeling weak and uneducated. *I AM WHO I AM? This wasn't in the names of God we studied earlier. Is God speaking in riddles because He is annoyed by Moses's question?* I felt the very same way the first time I read that passage.

I love the way Louie Giglio explained this passage in his bestselling book *I Am Not but I Know I AM: Welcome to the Story of God*:

> In English the name *I AM* translates into the verb *to be*. Or more simply, *be*.
>
> Therefore, God's name is *BE*.

I AM = I BE. Not great grammar I know, but powerful theology.

God knew it was imperative for Moses to know who He was—that He was *I AM*. *I AM* is the present tense, active form of the verb *to be.* As God's name, it declares that He is unchanging, constant, unending, always present, always God....

And God's name still is *I AM.*[3]

God is the great I AM. He is the ever-being God who is present when we fail, when we fear, and when we are shackled by our frailty. He "is the same yesterday, today and forever" God (Heb. 13:8). He is as present with us today as He was with Moses in the dusty desert of Horeb. He was present when Moses's mother placed him in the basket, when Moses killed the Egyptian, and when Moses fled to Midian. God used every experience in Moses's life to prepare him for what he was about to do.

He is the ever-being God who is present when we fail, when we fear, and when we are shackled by our frailty.

God isn't looking at your degrees, or lack of, to determine if you are a worthwhile possibility. He found the educated (Moses, Luke, and Paul) just as worthy as the uneducated (fishermen John, Peter, and Andrew). If God doesn't determine our value to His kingdom based on our schooling, why should we?

As God formed Moses in his mother's womb, God placed *deliverer* potential in his DNA. Moses's potential was always there, but not yet visible. It was possible, yet not actual. In this conversation, God was trying to show Moses what He had always seen: that Moses was a worthwhile possibility. However, Moses needed a little more convincing.

Frailty: Lack of Communication Skills

In Exodus 4:10, Moses revealed another of his frailties. Yes, after all of God's words of reassurance and promise of success, Moses was brave enough to ask another question. I must say, I love how the *New Living Translation* records the question: "But Moses pleaded with the LORD, 'O Lord, I'm not very good with words. I never have been, and I'm not now, even though you have spoken to me. I get tongue-tied, and my words get tangled.'" Perhaps you want to underline or highlight the word "pleaded."

Moses had just seen God perform some pretty miraculous wonders. (Don't worry. We will talk about the amazing wonders later in the chapter.) Yet he wasn't moved. He earnestly tried to convince God, this time with a very specific reason, why he was not the man for the job.

I have conversations like this with God more often than I care to admit. With honest sincerity, and great self-examination, I present to God why I can't possibly be the person He wants for the job. I imagine God sitting patiently on His royal throne, in His regal splendor, looking into the far, faraway distance, uttering, "Uh-huh. Yes. I hear you." Aren't we so blessed by His amazing, patient grace?

God knew Moses was fully equipped for this assignment, and He was prepared to pick up the slack of Moses's lack. What Moses remembered was the man he used to be: the man in the palace. Toned, educated, eloquent, and well represented. He also realized he hadn't used those skills in over forty years. He no longer spoke to royalty; now he spoke to sheep. He was no longer a who's who; now he was a not-anymore.

Some Bible scholars suggest that Moses had developed a speech impediment, perhaps a stutter. I've spent a lot of time speaking and teaching over the last fifteen years. With each passing year, my communication skills improve. But there are still those rare occasions when my tongue is so thick with southern that, in the moment, I have to backtrack and try again. When we don't exercise certain skills, we lose them, so this suggestion of a stutter is plausible. Personally, I ride the fence on the issue and try not to get lost in the forest for the trees. The bottom line is, Moses did not feel his skills were well developed enough to accurately and clearly communicate to God's people, much less to Pharaoh. But God was having none of that. He had a quick, sharp retort for brother Moses.

> Then the LORD asked Moses, "Who makes a person's mouth? Who decides whether people speak or do not speak, hear or do not hear, see or do not see? Is it not I, the LORD? Now go! I will be with you as you speak, and I will instruct you in what to say." (Ex. 4:11–12 NLT)

It is very apparent that God was reaching His boiling point with Moses. He'd promised victory. He'd promised a return. He'd promised His presence, and now He promised His words. Even with all these promises, Moses still felt like he was lacking.

When we submit our lack to the One who supplies for all our needs according to His riches in glory in Christ Jesus (Phil. 4:19) and has provided everything we need for godly living (2 Pet. 1:3), our frailties will no longer be a cross we have to bear. They will be treasures we can lay at His feet, trusting that He has the power to make us strong enough to accomplish all that He has planned for us.

What about you? Where are you in your conversation with the Lord about the assignment He has for you? Has God confirmed your calling and assured you of His presence, yet you still doubt your value and skill set? Let me encourage you to search the Scriptures; there's a verse for everything. I encourage you to continue to ask God questions and seek His answers.

Ask God questions and seek His answers.

Frailty: Lack of Confidence

In my day, I was an excellent pitcher. The mound and the plate were my dance floor. High and slow. The ball would drop at the back-inside corner of the zone, the umpire would yell "Strike," and the batter's mouth would fall open in disbelief. Those were glory days! I had all the confidence needed to play on a no-cut team—the church team, the team everyone makes regardless of their skill. However, I couldn't muster up enough confidence to try out for my school team. I had the skill and the experience but lacked the courage. Not trying is one of my biggest regrets. Softball wasn't the end-all-be-all and would have never become a career, but the not trying fueled the fire of self-doubt. Oh, what I would say if I could go back and talk to younger me!

Softball tryouts were the first of many things I didn't attempt. School leadership teams. School cheerleading. School dramas, which I totally would have rocked, because I can do some drama, friends! I remember when I finally got the courage to try out for the church ensemble. My confidence was getting stronger. I was growing in the Lord and had been asked to sing church solos for the Sunday-night and Wednesday-night services, so I thought it was time to take the risk.

My fifty-year-old brain can't recall what song I selected for my audition, but I remember times of putting the cassette (for those who aren't familiar, a cassette was a small plastic device that played recorded music off magnetic tape) in my player, pressing play, and singing into my hairbrush. The cassette went with me in my car too. As I drove, I belted out the tune like I was center stage in a coliseum full of hundreds of people who had paid to see me perform. Doug was the sound guy at our church, and he was kind enough to meet me one evening so I could rehearse onstage with the mic. Oh, I was ready. I was gonna rock this audition and be part of the "elite" young ensemble.

Audition night came. Audition night passed. I was not selected. And all of you girls say, "Awwww." (Emphasize it with a big southern drawl for effect, please.)

In hindsight, the real misfortune wasn't getting passed over for the ensemble. The worst part of the experience was allowing Satan, the enemy, to keep his foothold in my thought life. He taunted me for years, each time I entertained the notion of trying for something. He would roll out the scripts. *You aren't good enough. You don't have the look. If you were in the "in group" you would have made the ensemble.*

Never try for anything again. It's better just to accept that you aren't good enough, and then you don't ever have to risk crushed confidence and dashed hopes again.

We are a worthwhile possibility to God; He has a lot invested in our future.

Have you heard such things from the father of lies (John 8:44)? I feel sure the same liar who whispers in our ear and plays on our weaknesses was messing with Moses. He doesn't want us to enjoy the freedom Jesus died to give or to live out the plan God has for us. "For we are God's handiwork, created in Christ Jesus to do good works, which God prepared in advance for us to do" (Eph. 2:10). We are a worthwhile possibility to God; He has a lot invested in our future. God chose you and me for a good work, and He chose Moses for a good work. Moses just needed a little more convincing. In reading God's response, it seems Moses might have taken the situation one step too far. Here's the final excerpt from their conversation. Hold on to your hats, girls. God's reply may shock you.

> But Moses said, "Pardon your servant, Lord. Please send someone else."
> Then the LORD's anger burned against Moses and he said, "What about your brother, Aaron the Levite? I know he can speak well. He is already on his way to meet you, and he will be glad to see you." (Ex. 4:13–14)

I love so many things about this exchange; I don't know where to start. God got frustrated with all of Moses's questions and insecurities, but I love this conversation! I love that Moses wasn't confident. I love that Moses needed a lot of reassurance. I love that he left nothing unsaid between him and God. The two-verse dialogue tells us so much about our heavenly Father:

- We can keep asking God questions.
- God does get angry with His children, yes, but He also works with us in His anger.
- The questions we ask don't turn Him away.
- God is very patient.

The Lord was angry with Moses, but it's obvious His affection for Moses didn't change. Moses's questions didn't change God's mind about His choice for the task. We know, if we have read through the rest of the story, that God still used Moses to lead the people. In fact, I believe God felt compassion for Moses's plight. After all, He told Moses that his brother Aaron could assist him.

God's so pro-us!

A new job is always easier to adjust to with a friend by your side. God said to Moses, "You shall speak to him and put words in his mouth; I will help both of you speak and will teach you what to do. He will speak to the people for you, and it will be as if he were your mouth and as if you were God to him" (Ex. 4:15–16). Did you notice who would be doing the talking? God's compassion and caring about everything that concerns His children is overwhelming. Even in His anger, He showed his love and care for Moses. God's so pro-us! If only we'd trust Him and release the power our frailties have over us, we would be able to see all God can do through those things we see as weaknesses.

How the Lack Loses Its Power

We've addressed and assessed Moses's questions but missed a show-and-tell demonstration tucked in the middle of his inquiries. God reveals His mighty power while teaching us a very valuable lesson: what we hold on to tightly is often what holds us back.

Might I be bold for a moment? I want to be very careful to say what I have to say with sensitivity. If we don't properly deal with our frailties, they can become such a huge part of who we are that freedom apart from them is frightening. Our frailties can even become comfortable to us. Hang in there with me.

Most of us like to know what to expect; knowing provides security. We can deal with what we know; it's the unknown that freaks us out and causes a panic attack. Living with failure, fear, frailties, and faults (coming in chapter 5), we know something about what to expect. However, handling our frailties in a godly way means that what has held us back loses its control and power, leaving us in uncharted waters. Freedom is oh-so-wonderful, but it is also very scary. We don't know what is going to happen or how we are going to respond. Freedom is waiting; we just have to let go and watch what God does, like Moses did.

What we hold on to tightly is often what holds us back.

In Exodus 4, God asked Moses to let go of his staff. A staff, also known as a crook, is extremely important to a shepherd. Not only does it help a shepherd sustain his balance while walking on uneven terrain, the long, straight end is valuable for fending off predators in the wild. He uses the curved end to clear out underbrush, herd the sheep, and pull a wandering ewe back in line with the herd. Moses spent countless hours in the meadowlands and desert places keeping up with sheep. The crook no doubt had become a source of comfort.

> Moses answered, "What if they do not believe me or listen to me and say, 'The LORD did not appear to you'?"
>
> Then the LORD said to him, "What is that in your hand?"
>
> "A staff," he replied.
>
> The LORD said, "Throw it on the ground."
>
> Moses threw it on the ground and it became a snake, and he ran from it. Then the LORD said to him, "Reach out your hand and take it by the tail." So Moses reached out and took hold of the snake and it turned back into a staff in his hand. (Ex. 4:1–4)

Moses saw God's power when he let go. The very thing (failure, fear, frailty, or fault) we hold on to will be the very thing God uses in our life to display His power. I'm living proof, dear one. This one, who was afraid to try, applied to be part of the speaker team at Proverbs 31 Ministries in 2003, and was accepted. This one, who couldn't spell her way out of a paper bag, has published three books and two Bible studies. This one, who at one time had never read the whole Bible on her own, has led thousands of women and men worldwide through the whole Bible. Just like Moses, when I let go of what I knew and was comfortable with, God showed off, and has continued to show off. Holding on to comfortable would have kept me from seeing God's greatest work in my life.

Qualifying the Called

No one is too damaged or unskilled to join God in His work. God is more concerned about our commitment than our qualifications. In her book *Hope ... the Best of Things*, Joni Eareckson Tada tells of when she imagines speaking to Jesus in heaven while in her wheelchair. "The weaker I was in that thing [my wheelchair], the harder I leaned on you. And the harder I leaned on you, the stronger I discovered you to be. It never would have happened had you not given me the bruising of the blessing of that wheelchair."[4] Henry Blackaby says, "The reality is that the Lord never calls the qualified; He qualifies the called."[5]

It often takes us getting to the "end of ourselves" living with our frailty to open our hands and let go of that frailty. God sometimes makes us hit an all-time low of struggling in our frailties so that we can surrender them and see what He can do with them.

No one is too damaged or unskilled to join God in His work.

As we surrender our frailties, God works in our life to enact our potential and engage us in His work. Isn't this the desire of everyone who follows Him?

Reflecting on What God Can Do with My Frailty

1. I realize this may be difficult, even if it takes a day or two, but spend some quiet time with the Lord and allow Him to identify your frailty or frailties. Surrender each frailty to His care, and use this prayer as a starting place.

> *Lord, You formed me in my mother's womb with [name the frailty]. I don't know why You made me this way or created the circumstance for me to have [name the frailty]. From today forward I trust You to use my [name the frailty] for Your glory and my good. Help me see the good so my faith can be strengthened and others will see Your work in me.*

2. How has God shaped your life through your frailty?

3. It's one thing to identify your weaknesses and trust God with them, but who wants to boast about them? Paul openly proclaimed his weaknesses: "But he said to me, 'My grace is sufficient for you, for my power is made perfect in weakness.' Therefore I will boast all the more gladly of my weaknesses, so that the power of Christ may rest upon me" (2 Cor. 12:9 ESV). "Boast" here is the Greek word *kauchaomai* (kow-khah'-om-ahee), which means "to one's advantage,

to the praise of one."[6] Paul is suggesting we use our weaknesses for praise. What are some ways you can use your frailties to praise and glorify God?

4. In John 8:44, Jesus identified Satan as the father of lies. "When he lies, he speaks his native language, for he is a liar and the father of lies." In what ways has Satan lied to you concerning your frailties? Look up James 4:7 in your Bible. List the steps to getting rid of Satan's influence in your life.

5. The Holy Spirit uses God's Word to encourage, convict, and challenge us in our faith. In what ways have the words of this chapter and the truths of God's Word changed your perspective of frailties?

Revealing My Potential

Use the space provided to respond to this prompt: What has God revealed to you about your frailties? How can you begin to let go of your frailties and live in the freedom God offers?

Possibility Profile: Meg

As a child I grew up in a church that did not allow their members to send their children to public school; each family was responsible for their children's education. My mother was mentally and physically incapable of homeschooling my siblings and myself. There were seven of us and we were all one year apart in age. I never got the basic elementary education, like learning to read, write, and do math above a fifth-grade level, due to the family God choose for me to be born into.

I was never confident in my education because I didn't have one. I worked at a fast-food place in the little community I grew up in as a teenager and young adult, and I loved every minute of it. I love to cook, always have and I guess I always will. I hated to run the cash register because I didn't know how to count change, but the sweet couple I worked for lovingly, without criticism, taught me how to count change.

I married someone who made enough money to support us without my having to get a job, but when our children became school age and I wanted them to go to private school, I had to find a job to pay for their education. Because of how I grew up, I did not want them to go to public school. So I found a job helping my best friend's husband with his bookkeeping. I knew very little about bookkeeping at the time, and even less about a computer, but I was eager to learn. And because he grew up in the same church that I did, he too was very patient with me.

My boss's accountants trained me on the software they used, and eventually I went to work for them as a bookkeeper for all of their clients. They were a new father-and-son accounting firm just starting up, and they had plenty of time and patience to train me. The funny thing about me getting that job was the education that both of them had and the lack of education I had. I became a born-again believer just a few years after I went to work for them, and it did not take me any time at all to realize that God had strategically placed me in this job.

I worked for them for eighteen years before my dear friend Wendy Pope called me one day to ask me if I would be interested in interviewing at Proverbs 31 Ministries for the bookkeeper position. It was my heart's desire to work in ministry after becoming a Christian, but I had no idea what that would look like. Of course, I went on the interview, and by the grace of God, I got the job.

I worked for Proverbs 31 for six years, then began to feel God calling me to quit my job there. I had no idea what I was going to do when I left there; I just knew it was what He was speaking to my heart. So, I gave my notice in faith that God would provide and direct me on what He wanted me to do next. I have had a strong feeling since becoming a Christian that I am supposed to be in ministry somehow, someway. So, I was really, really wanting Him to open up a door for me in some type of ministry.

The last day at Proverbs 31 was my first day working directly for Lysa TerKeurst. I only worked until 1:00 every day, so I walked out of the door at Proverbs 31 and into Lysa's house thirty minutes later. And guess what some of my first tasks were? Cooking—cooking for her vow renewal, her book-launch party, and the Proverbs 31 Christmas party. As I said earlier, I love to cook, and I love to minister to people by serving them. This was and is the perfect job for me; I could not be happier.

The reason I share all of my work experiences is to say that even though I did not get the education I needed and deserved as a child, God provided every job to give me the tools I would need on the journey He was taking me on to bring glory to Himself.

When I worked at the fast-food restaurant, God gave me confidence to learn new things and not be afraid of the public. The job with my best friend's husband led me to the accounting job that taught me how to be a great bookkeeper, and I also got more comfortable interacting with people. The job at Proverbs 31 taught me how to handle conflict, and I learned how to agree to disagree. I learned that everything I was thinking did not have to be said, and just because I thought it, didn't make it right. God also taught me how to respect and follow leadership the way His Word teaches us to follow leadership. God has allowed me to learn who I really am and that the personality I have was given to me by Him for a reason, and it's not bad.

This journey has not been easy, nor has it been cut and dried. At times I have had to beg God to reveal to me what He was trying to teach me or what He wanted me to do. I have had to learn to trust and obey a holy God who loves me and has my best interest at heart. He has shown me through this journey in my relationship with Him that there is nothing He can't or will not do in someone's life who will allow Him to be in full control, even when we don't understand. Our frailties are not frail to Him.

Our frailties are not frail to Him.

Chapter 5

What God Can Do through My Faults

Do my faults exclude me from God's plan?

*Faults: things that we have control over
but sometimes we allow to control us.*

Fodder for office gossip, small group prayer requests, and social media mayhem—faults are not something we readily want to talk about, unless we are pointing them out in another person. It's rare to find anyone willing to work to keep their flaws under control, much less admit them. Those who acknowledge their faults often do so only followed closely by a justification:

- *I was born this way; just ask my momma.*
- *This is what happens when you have a past as colorful as mine.*
- *This is who I am; like it or lump it.*
- *It's too late to change now.*
- *They bring out the worst in me.*

Why is it easier to talk about failure, fear, and frailties than our faults? Could it be we know people are more likely to offer sympathy, empathy, and forgiveness for the other issues as opposed to the judgment we often feel they direct our way for our faults?

Failure is a great teacher. Failing might evoke comments like these: "Chalk it up to inexperience." "God will use it for your good and His glory." "At least you tried."

What about admitting fear? Fear is a great reminder to turn to God. If you confess your fears, your friends might say something like this: "You're going to be okay." "Put your trust in God." "I read in a book that fear is only a sin when it becomes a way of life."

Then there are our frailties. Frailties can be great blessings. Those who know you might encourage you with words such as these: "God made you just the way you are, warts and all." "You are strongest when you submit your weakness to God." "Lean on Him and His Word."

But what happens when we reveal our faults?

Faults can quickly discredit our character and, when left unchecked, can lead to character destruction. Faults come in many shapes and sizes, and everyone has them, no matter who we are or where we are from. We could have a critical or negative nature, pride, or insecurities. Maybe you struggle with a temper like Moses sometimes did, or maybe you have trouble controlling your mouth like Wendy does. Yeah, I thought I'd go ahead and put one of my faults out there right at the beginning of this chapter, even though it makes me squirm. You know that feeling when you are red-faced, sweaty, and smelly after a workout and you pray you don't see anyone you know? Well, if you and I came face to face just now, I'd be red-faced and looking for a place to hide.

A Fault of Mine

The mouth is a powerful tool. James, the brother of Jesus, likened it to the small rudder of a ship:

> Or take ships as an example. Although they are so large and are driven by strong winds, they are steered by a very small rudder wherever the pilot wants to go. Likewise, the tongue is a small part of the body, but it makes great boasts. Consider what a great forest is set on fire by a small spark. (James 3:4–5)

In full red face, I confess, I've had to put out many a great fire started by the spark from my tongue. Not that it makes what I'm about to divulge any less reprehensible, but it's only on rare occasions that I have intentionally used my mouth to create a spark. My mind usually generates the great comebacks and witty quips after I walk away from the situation. I've often wished I was quick thinking in the moment. However, after maturing in my faith, I've realized my slow response time is actually a blessing—a protection of sorts, to keep me out of trouble.

But let me wipe the sweat from my brow and disclose what happens more often than not with my flame starter. It's those moments when I intentionally spew the sarcastic stealth bomb with a little head cock, a hand-on-the-hip stance, and a pursed lip added in for good measure that discredit my character and defame my witness.

You see, our faults are not sinful, unless or until they take control of us. And I have definitely been guilty of letting mine control me. Let me paint a picture for you. Looking at me and knowing my area of ministry, I bet you would assume that I am an extrovert brimming with confidence. One would have to be to stand in front of a room full of strangers to speak and teach the Bible, right? Well, not this T-shirt-and-leggings-wearing, no-makeup-on, three-day-hair homebody. Somewhere along the path I stopped being the confident girl who stood on the pitcher's mound, throwing one strike after another. Little by little, walking into a room of people, whether I knew them or not, became difficult.

I'm not exactly sure how or when my confidence went on the decline and I lost control of my mouth, but I did. As each year passed, and I watched others live my dream, or achieve what I wanted to achieve, I sat lower in the seat on the back row. Failure wore me down. Then one day, I noticed that I had become the funny one—the quick-witted one that people seemed to like to be around. With a quick jab here and a lengthy diatribe over there, I drew others to me. They thought I was funny. My humor became a sort of coping mechanism for my inferiority complex: *If I can't be like her, and I keep failing, at least I can be funny.*

Don't get me wrong, humor and laughter are wonderful. But when humor turns to biting sarcasm, that's when feelings get hurt. Oh, I wish I could share of a time in my past when my sharp tongue hurt someone, a time when I was younger in age and faith, a time when I didn't know better. I wish.

Our faults are not sinful, unless or until they take control of us.

Recently, within a month of completing this manuscript, I was on a speaking trip with some of my closest lifelong friends. You know those girls—the ones who knew you then, know you now, and still love you anyway. The trip was coming to an end, and as we prepared to leave, something was said—I honestly don't even remember what. We were all taking potshots at one another, but in a moment, I quickly snapped out an incredibly rude comeback, complete with head gyration and eye roll, aimed right at my closet and dearest friend, my bestie. (You've met her if you've read my book *Yes, No and Maybe.* She's the girl I met in preschool.) In an instant, the spark started a fire of hurt, pain, and regret. Without intention, my rudder had changed the direction of the group's conversation, and I frantically began to backpedal.

My propensity to talk has been with me since I uttered my first word. I'm sure at one time or another my parents had to think, *And we wanted her to learn to talk.* Talking too much or saying the wrong things has always been my weakness—a fault, something that is a part of me, and works for me, until I allow it take control, then it works against me.

It's imperative we recognize and admit our faults, then submit them to the Spirit's control and the power of the Word. Years ago, God intersected my fault with a truth that has changed me. "Help me, Lord, to keep my mouth shut and my lips sealed" (Ps. 141:3 TLB). Like my son, who is now nineteen, used to say, there's a verse for everything. In fact, the Bible has much to say about our mouths, and for people with control issues like me, this is good news.

> Whoever guards his mouth preserves his life; he who opens wide his lips comes to ruin. (Prov. 13:3 ESV)

Knowing Scripture won't make us faultless, but it will make us Spirit sensitive.

Perhaps my favorite of all the mouth verses is the one that gives the antidote for the sharp, careless tongue, "But the words you speak come from the heart—that's what defiles you" (Matt. 15:18 NLT). Jesus is saying it's what we put in our heart and mind that defiles or makes us common like everyone else, so put the right things in and the right things will come out. I believe if we examine all our faults through the lens and light of this scripture, we will find an antidote for each one. God's Word, planted deep in our heart and mind, along with our surrender to its power, are the remedies to counteract our faults.

Knowing Scripture won't make us faultless, but it will make us Spirit sensitive. I've known these scriptures for a while, and yet I still hurt my friend's feelings; but it didn't last. The Spirit quickened my heart; I confessed and sought forgiveness. Now that's power.

Faults don't disqualify us from working with God.

God's grace covers this fault of mine and invites me to be part of the ministry He is doing on this side of eternity. He has allowed me to bless Him and others with words in the pages of books and from the pulpit. Faults don't disqualify us from working with God, but they might delay God's plan. They haven't disqualified me, and even though he had a few, faults didn't disqualify Moses either.

Fault One

The existence of faults is not a sin in itself, but our faults can lead us into sin if we let them control our actions and attitudes. Faults in this way are similar to temptations—they represent a weak spot in our character that can cause us to disobey God and hurt others. Faults become problematic when we allow them to dictate our responses and use them as excuses to neglect God's plan for our life.

Moses had two main faults: one he surrendered to God, and one he allowed to control him.

Like me, Moses had a mouth problem, as we talked about in chapter 4; however, his issue was different from mine. Though Moses briefly allowed his speech problem to define his worthiness to serve as the leader of God's people, he eventually took command and led the Israelites right up to the Land of Promise. Let's refresh ourselves with a bit of the conversation Moses had with God on this matter. I selected the *Complete Jewish Bible* for our review. Notice the spelling of Moses's name and what word is used for Lord. You know that one now, don't you? Isn't learning God's Word so fun?!

Moshe said to ADONAI, "Oh, Adonai, I'm a terrible speaker. I always have been, and I'm no better now, even after you've spoken to your servant! My words come slowly, my tongue moves slowly." ADONAI answered him, "Who gives a person a mouth? Who makes a person [mute] or deaf, keen-sighted or blind? Isn't it I, ADONAI? Now, therefore, go; and I will be with your mouth and will teach you what to say." (Ex. 4:10–12 CJB)

My mouth problem is very different from that of Moses. His tongue moved slow, and mine? Well, it moves too fast. It's very interesting to read the various commentaries' explanations of Moses's "slow tongue." There isn't a consensus on this subject. Some experts define the speech problem as stuttering, slow processing, and slower to speak, while others theorize that Moses didn't feel confident speaking in front of crowds, that he had stage fright, you might say. The exact reason for his slow speech isn't known, but we can assume it was not a result of poor education. "Moses was educated in all the wisdom of the Egyptians and was powerful in speech and action" (Acts 7:22). It wasn't that Moses didn't know what to say, but rather that he was not able to or didn't have the confidence to communicate his response.

God knows our inner making: "You made all the delicate, inner parts of my body and knit them together in my mother's womb" (Ps. 139:13 TLB). Since He created us, He knows our failures, fears, frailties, faults, and yet still has a good plan for our life: "For we are God's handiwork, created in Christ Jesus to do good works, which

God prepared in advance for us to do" (Eph. 2:10). He knew Joni Eareckson Tada would be paralyzed, Moses wouldn't speak well, and He knows all about you too. As we say in the south, He loves and accepts you, warts and all.

Matthew Henry said in his commentary of Exodus 4:10, "God sometimes makes choice of those as his messengers, who have the least of the advantages of art or nature, that his grace in them may appear the more glorious. Christ's disciples were no orators, till the Holy Spirit made them such."[1] I like that, don't you?

God knows our inner making.

Something else I love about Moses's speech problem: nowhere in Scripture do we read about God removing this fault. Moses never spoke of his speech problem again. He continued to walk in obedience to God, allowing Aaron to speak until one day when things shifted.

In one of their visits to Pharaoh concerning the plagues, Moses found his voice and the confidence to speak to Pharaoh himself: "Moses said to Pharaoh, 'I leave to you the honor of setting the time for me to pray for you and your officials and your people that you and your houses may be rid of the frogs, except for those that remain in the Nile'" (Ex. 8:9).

Moses overcame what had overcome him. The potential that God had placed inside Moses as he was formed in his mother's womb was finally being recognized. Unfortunately, this isn't the case with his other fault. Moses didn't surrender his anger; he succumbed to it.

Fault Two

Bityah, Moses's adopted mother, turned from the wicked ways of idolatry of her father and her people. She obviously didn't share Pharaoh's hatred for the Hebrew nation, because she chose to bring a Hebrew baby into her home as well as to acquire a Hebrew wet nurse to care for him, which as God would have it, would be Moses's own birth mother. According to many of the experts, it is believed that Bityah kept Moses aware of his true identity and connected to his faith. Therefore, it stands to reason that after living forty years among Egyptians, he never felt Egyptian. This familial background explains why Moses felt anger when he saw his "brother" being brutalized. However, his anger over the injustice being done doesn't justify murder.

Exodus 2 is the first time we see Moses's character being discredited by his fault. He simply lost control—something I can relate to.

> One day, after Moses had grown up, he went out to where his own people were and watched them at their hard labor. He saw an Egyptian beating a Hebrew, one of his own people. Looking this way and that and seeing no one, he killed the Egyptian and hid him in the sand. (Ex. 2:11–12)

Moses's failure and his fault were exposed in the same life event. With a desire to help his fellow Hebrew out of a tough spot and punish the one responsible, he failed by committing murder and allowed his fault (anger) to take control of him. As we survey the major events in Moses's life, we see how the pieces of our fractured faith can overlap and how easily our eyes can lose sight of our worth, diminishing hope of ever being part of God's great plan for our life.

God sees us as worthwhile, full of potential, and longs to advance His great plan for our life.

I love that God doesn't pull the plug on His plan for us after just one occurrence of failure, one moment of fear, one fault gone rogue, or one frailty unsurrendered. If this were the case, Moses's story would have ended the day he killed the Egyptian. Instead, God continued to communicate and work with Moses, using the pieces of his fractured faith to advance God's great plan for His beloved Israel. No matter what we do, or don't do, God sees us as worthwhile, full of potential, and longs to advance His great plan for our life.

Throughout the story of Exodus, Moses demonstrated his short fuse. I feel quite certain leading an unruly, unfaithful, idolatrous group had to be trying. Their constant complaining of no food, no water, and endless wandering would be enough to unleash the fury of the greatest of saints. I heard someone once say it would be easy to be a Christian if it weren't for the people. And Moses certainly had his hands full of people, didn't he?

The Israelites were thirsty; walking around in the desert has that effect on you. As usual, when their needs weren't being met, the group complained to Moses and Aaron. Thirst was a hot button for God's people. On numerous occasions their displeasure turned to protest.

When they arrived at Marah after leaving Egypt, they complained about the water being too bitter. God instructed Moses to throw a branch in the water in order to remove the bitterness (Ex. 15:22–27). Later in their travels, they camped at Rephidim and again complained about being thirsty. This time, however, God gave Moses a different instruction. Will you underline the word "strike"?

> The LORD answered Moses, "Go out in front of the people. Take with you some of the elders of Israel and take in your hand the staff with which you struck the Nile, and go. I will stand there before you by the rock at Horeb. Strike the rock, and water will come out of it for the people to drink." So Moses did this in the sight of the elders of Israel. (Ex. 17:5–6)

With a strike of the rock, the quarreling ceased, and the people had water to drink. Moses went on to faithfully and with great patience lead the Israelites to the edge of the Promised Land. Finally, after forty years of wandering in the desert, eating manna, and wearing the same sandals (that never wore out), the wait was over. They were ready to enter Canaan, the Land of Promise. They were ready, but they were thirsty. "Now there was no water for the community, and the people gathered in opposition to Moses and Aaron. They quarreled with Moses and said, 'If only we had died when our brothers fell dead before the LORD!'" (Num. 20:2–3).

As with every other case of complaint, Moses and Aaron sought the Lord. They went to the Tent of Meeting (the place where the

Spirit of God dwelled) and humbled themselves before God to ask for direction. God was faithful to give *exact* instructions. Will you underline the word "speak"?

> Take the staff, and you and your brother Aaron gather the assembly together. Speak to that rock before their eyes and it will pour out its water. You will bring water out of the rock for the community so they and their livestock can drink. (Num. 20:8–9)

That is what God said. And this is what Moses did:

> So Moses took the staff from the LORD's presence, just as he commanded him. He and Aaron gathered the assembly together in front of the rock and Moses said to them, "Listen, you rebels, must we bring you water out of this rock?" Then Moses raised his arm and struck the rock twice with his staff. Water gushed out, and the community and their livestock drank. (Num. 20:9–11)

Will you underline the words "struck" and "twice"?

God's instructions to Moses were clear: "Speak to that rock." In the moment, Moses, rather than controlling his impatient anger, allowed his fault to control him. He struck the rock twice instead of speaking to it. Are you thinking what I'm thinking? What's the big deal? God told him on an earlier occasion to strike the rock, so he got mixed up. The water still gushed out.

Bible commentaries vary in their answer to "what's the big deal?" Let's face it: no one really knows except God, Moses, and Aaron. This is what we do know. Moses …

- spoke to the people when he was only supposed to speak to the rock (Num. 20:10)
- stood center stage as an equal to God, supposing he was partner to God's power (Num. 20:10–11)
- struck the rock twice, when he wasn't supposed to strike it even once (Num. 20:11)

God allowing Moses to "remove the bitterness" at Marah and strike the rock at Rephidim affirmed Moses as the people's leader with authority, and his staff as a conduit of God's power. The water issue at Kadesh was God's opportunity to display His power without Moses and the staff to this new generation of Israelites.

The older generation had been subjected to forty years of desert living and desert dying because they didn't believe God could conquer the "land of giants" of Canaan when they first arrived at the land's edge (Num. 14:26–30). God now had the opportunity to start fresh, so to speak, hopeful this new group would be more faithful than the one before. However, Moses lost control of his fault—his temper. He characterized God as angry and short-tempered rather than revealing Yahweh as holy and long-suffering, a God of compassion and their source of provision.

Moses had an exceptional history of obedience despite his fears, faults, frailties, and failures. However, this rock-banging incident was not one of his finest moments. Anger isn't wrong. In fact, none of our "Fs" are wrong; it's how we respond to them that brings blessing or discipline.

He should have pressed pause. In his haste and anger, he stole the glory that was due to God. God will not share His glory with another: "I am the LORD; that is my name! I will not yield my glory to another or my praise to idols" (Isa. 42:8). His perfect plan for us does not include sharing the spotlight. Our potential, the possibility He sees in us, is to be developed and spent on His kingdom, for His glory, not for our own gain. Moses paid a high price for his fault-gone-wrong.

There on the mountain that you have climbed you will die and be gathered to your people, just as your brother Aaron died on Mount Hor and was gathered to his people. This is because both of you broke faith with me in the presence of the Israelites at the waters of Meribah Kadesh in the Desert of Zin and because you did not uphold my holiness among the Israelites. Therefore, you will see the land only from a distance; you will not enter the land I am giving to the people of Israel. (Deut. 32:50–52)

I know what you are thinking. *Seriously? After all he did and everything he put up with, he makes one mistake and can't enter the Promised Land? Isn't that a bit harsh?* I understand your sentiments; really, I do. I won't pretend to have some profound explanation. Our God has secrets no one knows (Deut. 29:29). He has ways that are higher and more far-reaching than our ways. And if Moses didn't complain, stomp his feet, and act a fool about the situation, then who are we to question God?

Our God has secrets no one knows.

Moses's disobedience and single act of glory-stealing didn't sever his relationship with God. Oh, how I wish we could read the final chapters of Deuteronomy together. God continued to speak to Moses, and Moses continued to obey God. What great hope and a powerful example of following God we have in these chapters! God's response offers hope that our disobedience won't disqualify us from His plan. Moses shows us to trust and obey when things go differently than planned, rather than recoil and rebel. He owned his sin and dealt with the consequence.

Our disobedience won't disqualify us from God's plan.

Moses's continued obedience earned him a blessing no one else in the Bible received: "And Moses the servant of the LORD died there in Moab, as the LORD had said. He buried him in Moab, in the valley opposite Beth Peor, but to this day no one knows where his grave is" (Deut. 34:5–6). His life was a life well spent—one of flaws and failures, frailty and fear. Yet God loved him so much, He buried him in a place only He knows. I can only imagine what an amazing graveside service that was.

What Faults Can Do

We've seen Moses's faults exposed, dissected, and pulled apart, something most of us would agree is not what we'd sign up for. Our faults, like our failures, fears, and frailties, can have power over us. Moses could have allowed his faults to keep him down, but then he would have never experienced years of walking with God. In faithfulness, with fear and trembling, he walked with God and learned what faults *can* do.

Faults *can* lead us to live under the Spirit's control or cause us to lose control. In the Old Testament, God chose to place His Spirit upon certain individuals: Saul (1 Sam. 11:6), David (1 Sam. 16:13), and Samson (Judg. 14:6) are a few examples. Moses didn't have the Holy Spirit in him like the aforementioned men, but he had God's presence with him. The Spirit of God dwelled on the mercy seat in the Holy of Holies of the Tabernacle (Lev. 16:2). The Spirit also led the people by fire and by cloud through the wilderness (Ex. 13:21). God freely talked with Moses.

Faults can lead us to live under the Spirit's control or cause us to lose control.

Everyone who confesses Jesus as Savior has the Holy Spirit living inside of them (1 Cor. 6:19; 1 John 4:2). Basically, we are a flesh tent, indwelled with the Spirit of God. Talk about opposites. Like a stretched rubber band, our flesh pulls us one way and the Spirit pulls us the other.

The apostle Paul explained it like this, "I don't understand why I act the way I do. I don't do what I know is right. I do the things I hate" (Rom. 7:15 CEV). You see, we aren't meant to lead and direct our own lives, and when we try to be in control, we easily lose control. God gave us the gift of the Holy Spirit to help us. His job is to teach, correct, and train (2 Tim. 3:16)—to reveal what is hidden so we can live up to our potential. We experience His power and guidance when we submit our control to His teaching rather than following our own thinking.

You see, we aren't meant to lead and direct our own lives.

The writer of Proverbs advises us not to be wise in our own eyes (Prov. 3:7). And he shows us more of his great wisdom in Proverbs 3:5–6. One of my favorite translations of these verses is The Passion Translation. I am quite certain that you are going to love it too.

> Trust in the Lord completely,
> and do not rely on your own opinions.
> With all your heart rely on him to guide you,
> and he will lead you in every decision you make.
> Become intimate with him in whatever you do,
> and he will lead you wherever you go.

As we learn to trust the Lord, we will value His thoughts and opinions more than our own. Soon, allowing Him to have control of our lives will be as natural as breathing. There may be the occasional self-in-control moment, but they will be fewer and further between. The peace that accompanies surrender will fill us. We will have an overwhelming desire to do whatever it takes to maintain that peace.

Faults *can* cost, so pause and do some calculations before you act. Quick responses and impulsive behavior can be expensive. Relationships. Employment. Right standing in the community. Moses lost his invitation to the Promised Land. And me? Well, I initiated a middle school scrap with a lifelong friend. My anger didn't cause me to strike a rock, but my mouth spewed some hurtful words that struck my friend. (Yes, again my mouth hurt a friend. I told you I'm a mess!) The drama is too ridiculous to share the play-by-play; honestly it is. And in respect for all those involved, I will spare you the details.

Faults can cost, so pause and do some calculations before you act.

This event happened the same weekend as my earlier word-spewing story. Remember that my friends joined me one weekend as I traveled to speak. Being enclosed in a vehicle over a long period of time, with little sleep, can wear on you. In an intense moment, my fault took control. Words were exchanged, and silence fell. At the time, my mind couldn't recall my mouth's life verse, "Set a guard, O LORD, over my mouth; keep watch over the door of my lips" (Ps. 141:3 NKJV). However, in the middle of my first speaking session, the Holy Spirit helped me remember. Yes, while I was standing before a crowd teaching, the Teacher taught me. My spirit was grieved. *OUCH!*

Immediately after the amen, I followed the Spirit's direction, addressed the issue with my friend, and reconciled. I'd love to say my fault will *never* take control of me again, but I know that's not possible. I mean, really, this was twice in just one trip. There are times when the stretch of the flesh pulls and snaps. We just have to regroup, repent to God, resubmit ourselves to Him, and reconcile with others. Nothing is worth the cost of letting our faults be in control, nothing.

Faults *can* shape our character, so determine what look you are going for. I wish I could say my mouth was the only place my life paralleled that of our friend Moses. Not only has my mouth taken control of me, but my temper has as well. The result has been doors slammed, commands barked, and holes put in walls—one from smashing the doorknob because my daughter wouldn't take a nap and the other from my foot because my son wouldn't obey. All of this happened because I let my fault take control. I wonder whether Moses ever looked back on his rock-banging episode with regret. Over a decade has passed, and I still cry when I think of my actions.

Faults can shape our character, so determine what look you are going for.

My outbursts were shaping my character. My children were being raised by a woman with a short fuse, who found belittling an acceptable form of communication and passive-aggressive behavior a coping mechanism for the hurt in her heart. Oh, friend, my entire body grieves as I share this ugly, ugly side of me.

My eruptions weren't constant; I threw in enough Jesus and Bible to confuse my people. At bedtime we'd say prayers and have devotions, then the next day something silly would set me off, and the door slamming and yelling would begin. It was shortly after I put my heel through the wall that I realized what was happening. My temper was spinning me out of control, and I needed to be under the Spirit's control if I wanted my character to look anything like the Jesus I was preaching to my children.

In humility, and great humiliation, I confessed my anger to God and asked Him to help me overcome it. Though my children were young, I asked them to forgive me too. Surrendering control *of* my life to the Spirit *in* my life was the best thing I could have ever done for my character. Slowly, through submission to His direction and the power of His Word, my life began to calm down and my character changed to reflect Jesus. Most days now, in moments that would have normally sent me sideways before, I can surrender the power and pause so I don't strike the rock. Or the wall.

We never completely overcome all our failures, fears, frailties, and faults, but we can allow God to repair our fractured faith through the work of the Holy Spirit and His Word. It's up to us to introduce our "Fs" to our great and powerful God. We know through Moses that when we lay our weaknesses down, we see exactly how strong our God can be through them.

It's up to us to introduce our "Fs" to our great and powerful God.

Moses's life was one full of potential, even if he couldn't see it. He was born with a death decree assigned to him, yet his life was sovereignly protected in order for him to fulfill the plan God designed specifically for him.

It would be easy to label Moses a failure and assume that, since he wasn't permitted to enter the Promised Land, he didn't reach his full potential. I beg to differ. Moses submitted to God every step of the way. He demonstrated humility, trust, and faithful service. His life was well spent. God planned for him to lead the people to Canaan, and he did. And because of his example, three of the world's major religions consider Moses a portrait of a godly leader.

You and I are like Moses. We were also born full of potential with a death decree assigned to us, but God sacrificed His Son to satisfy the death penalty associated with our sin. He did this so we could fulfill our part in His story. You might not feel full of potential right now. Perhaps you aren't experiencing a rush of worthiness. Maybe what you've read has rehashed failures you'd forgotten, fears you buried, frailties you are embarrassed by, or faults you didn't know you had. If so, you are right where God wants you—humbled and ready for marching orders.

Reflecting on What God Can Do with My Faults

1. Faults are things that we have control over but sometimes we allow to control us. At the beginning of this chapter, I listed a few excuses we offer to compensate for our faults. Review the list. Which excuse do you most identify with? What other excuses do you offer?

2. Psalm 19:12 says, "But who can discern their own errors? Forgive my hidden faults." Write a prayer asking God to help you recognize the parts of your character that don't align with His. You can use Psalm 19:12 as a starting place.

3. We can't leave our faults unchecked *until* they discredit our character. It's imperative to live in tandem with the Holy Spirit and God's Word so we can align our faults with the character of God. Look up Galatians 5:22–23. Write out the fruit of the Spirit, and identify which fruit sharply conflicts with your fault.

4. The Passion Translation of Proverbs 3:5–6 says, "Trust in the Lord completely, and do not rely on your own opinions. With all your heart rely on him to guide you, and he will lead you in every decision you make. Become intimate with him in whatever you do, and he will lead you wherever you go." How can you change your actions to imitate Christ in what you do?

5. How have your faults cost you?

Revealing My Hidden Potential

Use the space provided to respond to the following prompt: What has God revealed to you about your faults? What faults are you allowing to control you?

Possibility Profile: Linda

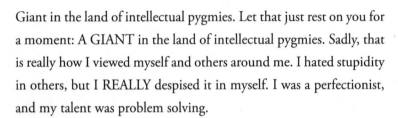

Giant in the land of intellectual pygmies. Let that just rest on you for a moment: A GIANT in the land of intellectual pygmies. Sadly, that is really how I viewed myself and others around me. I hated stupidity in others, but I REALLY despised it in myself. I was a perfectionist, and my talent was problem solving.

My identity was wrapped up in what and how I could accomplish through my intellect. Looking back, I didn't even realize how much of myself was defined by what I could figure out and the problems I could solve. It really isn't that my intellect or problem-solving abilities were a problem, but it was in how I was using them in the world around me. At the time, I was working in product development in the field of corporate engineering. I loved what I did, and I was successful at it. To the world, I appeared to have it all together—climbing the corporate ladder, married with children, serving in church. I had arrived.

BUT God.

At the time, I was serving God in the church and community, and I was always willing to share my faith at work. I was even leading Bible studies and doing my daily devotions. And all the while, God was slowly and sweetly pouring out so much grace. He was chiseling away anything that was not like Him. My intellect, pride, and problem solving came face to face with who God really is, and to get right down to it, I was not using my talents and abilities for God's glory, even if in my mind I was.

Oswald Chambers defines amateur providence as one trying to play God's role in the lives of others. Little did I realize at first in my walk with God that my ability to solve problems in the lives of others was my being an amateur providence to them. Rather than praying for the person's needs, and pointing them to God, I would solve their problems. Instead of the person seeing God work in their midst by going to God with their problems, they would implement my solution and never have an encounter with God. Their faith would not grow, and they would miss seeing God's faithfulness in their lives. I shudder thinking of how I misused the very talents and abilities God gave me, and all the missed opportunities to see God do the unimaginable. The realization of this was a slow process. God never forced His hand as He rightfully could have. Rather, He used a simple prayer I was asking for my children and a verse and had them collide.

As great as my intellect is, I have always struggled with memorizing scripture word for word. Yet ironically, God introduced me to a song that allowed me to memorize a very specific verse: Proverbs 3:5–6. (If you don't know it, this will make you laugh, and if you know it, you are probably already laughing out loud.) "Trust in the LORD with all your heart and lean not on your own understanding; in all your ways submit to him, and he will make your paths straight." Did you catch that? NOT on your OWN understanding, your intellect?

Then a few years later, right after 9/11, my prayers became more urgent for my children's salvation. My career was taking off, and I absolutely loved what I was doing, but the Spirit began to make me unsettled at work. I can't even put my finger on what it was specifically now, but I got the sense I was supposed to make a dramatic change. As it would happen, there were layoffs occurring at my company. I told God (don't you just love how *I* was telling God this?), "God, if You want me to leave this place, just have me laid off, and I'll do whatever You want."

However, being laid off would have been something that happened to me, out of my control. Quitting, on the other hand, walking away from my career and all that it entailed, would be my giving up the control of my talents, abilities, and that which was my very heart's desire and my identity, and instead choosing to be obedient to God, trusting HIM with what He wanted me to do.

Please realize that quitting is not something that this perfectionist does! Tied up in my intellect was my pride and much of my identity and my desire for control. I held on to that as a precious idol, but once I opened my hands to God, and gave Him my talents and abilities of intellect and problem solving, God took away the taste and desire for all that I had in the corporate world. It now was time to use all that He had given me for His glory.

Little did I realize, my choice to "retire" from engineering would fulfill God's desire to use me as an instrument in answering the prayer I had for my children. By my surrendering that which I loved, and changing my vocation location to be at home, I would learn to humbly use my intellect to teach and guide my children to know Jesus. But that was just the beginning of how God would work, and where God would take me.

In the midst of all that God was doing to expose my true potential, He was revealing what I was doing when I was the providence of my talents and abilities. Excellent problem solving allowed me to control the world around me. Removing problems and doing everything myself and not asking for help were all part of the idol of control I had created for myself. When I bow to this idol, I am really saying that I do not trust God in His sovereignty to work in the midst of my own life or in the lives of those I love dearly. Let that sink in. I was saying, "God, I don't trust You! I don't trust You to provide, to work in the lives of my children so they know You deeper, and that Your plan and solution are better (immeasurably more) than mine."

Instead of solving everyone's problems, including mine, I had to learn to just stop doing everything, be still, and ask God to work in the situation. It is at this point of total and utter surrender of a situation to God that I have witnessed miracles and God's awesome work. He faithfully and lovingly works on behalf of us, to aid and assist me and others in ways that I could never have imagined. I love that I am not the only one who has experienced this.

In Exodus 18, we see that Moses had the ability to problem-solve, and people were lining up day and night to get his wise counsel. Thankfully, Moses had a loving father-in-law, Jethro, who saw not only the potential frustration of the people but also the exhaustion of Moses. Jethro wisely counseled Moses to get assistance from others to take the burden to solve and mitigate the day-to-day problems and concerns of the people of Israel. Bringing others to serve alongside us with their talents and abilities also lets us see God working through the lives of others and encourages our faith.

God has taken my faults and equipped me so that I might be able to serve Him in ways I never imagined. God is having me use my desire to problem-solve and my intellect to assist others in their ministry to serve God. He helps me to see the hidden potential in other people and has me encourage and gracefully refine them, so that they might use their gifts and abilities for God's glory.

The process to get here was not a straight path, but rather a meandering stroll with the occasional off-roading, unexpected joy ride you can only have by knowing God. I know none of this would have ever happened had I not been encouraged to be in the Word daily, learning about who God was and His metanarrative. Reading a chapter or more a day allowed me to have God expose my faults and reveal who He was. But even more, through my obedience to what is in the Word, I discovered what my hidden potential was and who I am in Him.

Chapter 6

What God Can Do through My Future

Can I move forward?

The last chapter of a book is always the hardest for me to write. It's like saying good-bye to good friends. This closing is especially difficult. I'm thinking of you, your heart, raw and exposed, and how you might be reeling in thought. We've talked about some hard stuff, haven't we? Maybe you are asking the same questions I'm asking: *Where do I go from here, Lord? How do I move from here? Can I move from here? My ugliness is all out there—now what?*

Let me suggest we check back in with Moses. Examining his life has gotten us this far; it's only fitting we see how everything played out for him. We already know his disobedience and glory-thievery prohibited his entrance to the Promised Land. After he received this devastating news, he continued to lead the people, which I personally find amazing. Don't you? As he wrapped up his assignment, he offered the people some parting remarks. His pep talk outlines how God's people should proceed, and I think we can glean much from his words.

Recommit to the Covenant

"Therefore, obey the terms of this covenant so that you will prosper in everything you do" (Deut. 29:9 NLT). "Covenant" is a big churchy word that could come across as intimidating. A covenant is a conditional agreement between people. When God's people walked out of the bondage of slavery, God established His law with them. The Hebrew word for "covenant" as represented to God's rescued beloved ones is *berith* (ber-eeth'). The Mosaic covenant was a divine constitution given to Israel with promises on the condition of obedience and penalties for disobedience. Its namesake was Moses simply because

Moses received the law and communicated the agreement with the people. Pardon me while I go all Old Testament on you for a minute. Hang there, I promise this is important.

The covenant included the Law and the sacrificial system for the atoning of sin. There would be a high priest established from the line of Levi (one of Jacob's sons, of the twelve tribes). This high priest would be the only one permitted to enter the Holy of Holies, or the most special room in the Tabernacle, to seek reconciliation for the sins of the people. He alone would offer the blood sacrifice of a perfect lamb to atone for their sins. The conditions of the covenant were simple: the people agreed to obey God, and God, in turn, agreed to protect and provide for them. The people agreed (Ex. 19:8).

In order to move forward, a recommitment was necessary.

In these, his final remarks, Moses reminded the people of this covenant and its importance. He thoroughly reviewed the promise of prosperity and blessings on those who obeyed, as well as the curses that would befall anyone who disobeyed (Deut. 28:1–29:1). Moses knew he would not be with this new generation of people as they trod the soil of their land, and that the recap was necessary. This peek at the past reminded them all of the covenant God had established, as well as how they would flourish in the new land. In order to move forward, a recommitment was necessary.

Our brief tread in the deep waters of the old covenant is necessary so we can marvel in the new covenant. Oh, the wonderful and match-less grace of the new covenant! Those who have confessed their sin and called Jesus Savior are partakers in this amazing new agreement. Unlike the old, we don't have an obligatory covenant with God, a "you do this and I'll do that" relationship. We believe in Jesus, we repent, we receive forgiveness, and the realization of His love, mercy, and grace compels us to live our life according to His Word and His ways.

The sacrificial system and the law were completely satisfied (fulfilled) by the perfect, spotless sacrifice, Jesus. "Don't misunderstand why I have come. I did not come to abolish the law of Moses or the writings of the prophets. No, I came to accomplish their purpose" (Matt. 5:17 NLT). When Jesus died, access to the Holy of Holies, once given only to the high priest, was given to everyone. The curtain separating the Holy Place from the most Holy Place, God from man, was torn from top to bottom (Matt. 27:51). We can talk to God anytime, anywhere, about anything. Perhaps the most significant of all differences in the two covenants is this: the old covenant ended in death and the new covenant ends in everlasting life.

Though we aren't bound by the law now, we should respect it as a means to point us to the need of a Savior and to help us live a life of holiness. "For it is written: 'Be holy, because I am holy'" (1 Pet. 1:16). Without God's law and His Word, we can't see where we fall short in our pursuit of holiness. Therefore, we must recommit ourselves to recognizing the awesomeness of Jesus's sacrifice and gift of salvation. We need to determine to submit ourselves to the truths of God's Word and their work in our lives so we can live fully in our potential just as Moses did. In order to move forward, a recommitment is necessary.

Review anew the covenant that God made with you through His Son, Jesus. There are no conditions you have to meet and no need to negotiate a better deal because, "This makes Jesus the guarantor of a better covenant" (Heb. 7:22 ESV).

Maybe this idea of a better covenant is new to you. Maybe you thought following Jesus was all about rules and dos and don'ts. If so, you'd be in good company. I've met non-Christians, new Christians, and seasoned Christians who have all had that same thought. But I'm happy to set you straight—following Jesus is about freedom. It is about an endless supply of love, mercy, and grace that you did nothing to deserve and can do nothing to lose.

Have you entered into the new covenant with Jesus? Have you confessed your sin and asked Jesus to be your Lord and Savior? If you haven't, look over this prayer of confession and commitment and think about whether or not you are ready to accept the amazing gift of grace Jesus offers. And if you are already a Jesus follower, look at this prayer and think about what it means to recommit to Him.

Oh, God, I am a sinner. I confess that I have done wrong (Rom. 3:23). I now recognize that apart from Your grace I will spend eternity apart from You (6:23). Your Son died so that I can have eternal life (John 3:16), and I want to accept His free gift of salvation (Rom. 6:23). He was innocent and yet He died for me. Thank You for the gift of Your Word and the Holy Spirit to help me live the life Jesus died to give me. You formed me in my mother's womb. I am filled with potential that You placed inside me (Ps. 139:13). I want to live for You.

Oh, dear one, if you have prayed this prayer of salvation, or one like it, then all heaven is rejoicing over you: "In the same way, I tell you, there is rejoicing in the presence of the angels of God over one sinner who repents" (Luke 15:10). I want to celebrate too. My contact information is in the back of the book. Please stuff a piece of paper in the spine or paperclip the page to mark your place, and contact me through email or social media. Hallelujah! Praise His name!

The need to recommit to or accept the new covenant given to us through Jesus's death offers us the first step to moving forward and engaging our potential. Returning to God is the second step.

Return to God

In addition to all the curses and blessings that would come to Israel, God spoke a prophetic word through Moses about their future. Unfortunately, they would fall into a cycle of habitual disobedience and idolatry. (I wonder if this made Moses sad.) God would have no other choice but to subject them to the curses He had promised. The curses included being exiled to a foreign land for a period of seventy years. God fulfilled His word, not only with the blessings, but also with the justice.

He also promised to gather them back together and to change their hearts (Deut. 30:3, 6). This brings us to the beautiful promise of Deuteronomy 30:10. (I wonder if this made Moses smile.)

> The LORD your God will delight in you if you obey his voice and keep the commands and decrees written in this Book of Instruction, and if you turn to the LORD your God with all your heart and soul. (NLT)

God longs for His children to make the right choices and follow His will for their lives; however, He won't make us obey. Therefore, when we make poor choices, choosing sin rather than submission,

God will let the chips fall where they may and allow us to face the natural consequences of our sin. Like we see with the Israelites, and specifically Moses, He is a God of justice. He says what He means and means what He says. That being true, we can also count on this truth: God will restore relationship with His estranged children. His grace is greater than our sin, and His mercy can't miss us; both are waiting when we return to Him.

God's grace is greater than our sin, and His mercy can't miss us.

Many years ago, my soul was troubled for a long season. My marriage wasn't my happily-ever-after I thought it would be, my son had great educational needs that were taxing, and even though I was having a regular quiet time with the Lord every day, I felt exiled from Him. It was weird. My church attendance was regular, my service was consistent, and I went to weekly Bible study; and yet, I felt so far from God. To top off the spiritual fog, during this same season, I sensed God calling me into ministry. I had no idea what that looked like, I felt less than qualified to answer the call, and I thought I was far from having potential. Have you ever felt that way? You are doing all the right things, but something is wrong.

Early one morning my Bible reading took me to the book of Joel. Joel was a minor prophet writing to the people of Israel after they had turned away from God again after their seventy-year exile. I'll be honest, Joel is not a book I had ever read, much less studied. It's one of those small books of the Bible you have to look up in the table of contents. So, you can imagine my surprise when the Spirit began to poke my heart through the words of the book of Joel.

To you, LORD, I call, for fire has devoured the pastures in
the wilderness and flames have burned up all the trees of
the field. (Joel 1:19)

That was me, in a devoured and burned-up wilderness! God was
clearly giving me instructions. There weren't a lot of details, just *Call
to the Lord*. I know, this seems elementary, doesn't it? I had never really
considered calling on Him. I was in the mind-set that I could fix things.

Joel is a short book and I was intrigued—well, compelled—to
continue to read. When I got to 2:12–13, I sensed another instruction from the Lord. *You are in a dry, burned-up place? Your soul is
troubled? Call to Me and …*

> "Even now," declares the LORD,
> 		"return to me with all your heart,
> 		with fasting and weeping and mourning."
>
> Rend your heart
> 		and not your garments.
> Return to the LORD your God,
> 		for he is gracious and compassionate,
> slow to anger and abounding in love,
> 		and he relents from sending calamity.

Wow, He was speaking, but using words I did not understand.
Fasting? *I have to give up food?* Weeping and mourning? *I feel like
crying a lot, so I think I've got this part.* Rend? *Where's my dictionary?*
My heart was anxious as I tried to figure out what these verses meant.

As I reread them, I decided to focus on the parts I did understand. We often allow ourselves to become so paralyzed by what we don't understand that we don't live out what we do understand.

Return to Me.

God says the same phrase twice, and when He repeats Himself, we should certainly take notice. I had some time, so I decided to use some of the free online commentaries to determine the meaning of this passage. This link took me here, that link took me somewhere else, until I finally found some answers.

Rend means "to tear apart." It was customary in the day to display your grief and sorrow with loud weeping and the tearing of your garments. In doing so, everyone would know that something was going on with you. God was telling His people (and me) to feel remorseful over their sin but not to let everyone know about it. In other words, this is a private, not a public, issue. The only people involved are the returner and the Receiver. Just so you know, this rending is not a one-and-done deal; it is our daily response to sin. God wants our heart as pure as a human heart can be.

Little by little, my soul was lifted from the season of darkness. Confession really is good for the soul. The more time I spent in God's Word, the more confident I felt about saying yes to the call of ministry, the easier it was to trust God with all my "Fs," and the more secure I felt with God being in control. His ways, though higher, really are better than mine. When I lean on His understanding, the straight path leads to Him every time.

God is famous for taking the old and making it new. He longs to do new in you.

While we sit in the aftershock of all the Spirit has revealed to us in the first five chapters, we are faced with a choice: we can return to God or we can return to the way things were. I pray you choose the former. You are a worthwhile possibility to God, full of potential, waiting to be discovered. Pushing through the muck and mire of your failures, fears, frailties, and faults won't be easy, but it's far better than the way things are now. God wants to reveal what He can do through you. He's the Creator of the universe. He's famous for taking the old and making it new. He longs to do new in you: "See, I am doing a new thing! Now it springs up; do you not perceive it? I am making a way in the wilderness and streams in the wasteland" (Isa. 43:19).

He did a new thing in the lives of many people. Individuals who, like you and me, struggled with "Fs."

Person	Potential
Sara was impatient.	Mother to Isaac, who fathered Esau and Jacob.
Jacob was a cheater.	Father of the twelve tribes of Israel, God's people.
David had an affair.	A great king of Israel and a man after God's own heart.
Peter had a temper.	Leader and speaker, spreading the Christian faith.
Paul was a murderer.	Greatest evangelist of all time.

And this list could go on. There is no end to what God can do through a life surrendered to Him. God sees it in you, friend. He knows that you are a worthwhile possibility, and He is ready to reveal new things in you. What is your response? Are you ready to return? It doesn't matter where you've wandered or how far, today is the day to return. It's necessary to return to God so you can move forward.

Look for Your Burning Bush

God knew Moses before he was formed in his mother's womb. He knew every failure Moses would ever make, every fear he'd ever experience, every frailty he'd try to overcome, and every fault he'd allow to take over him. God knew it all, and yet He still chose Moses. And Moses chose to walk up to the burning bush.

There is no end to what God can do through a life surrendered to Him.

Look up. Moses rose above his failure to walk up to the burning bush and encounter God. Little did he know this step would be the first in many that would ensure his potential would be revealed, visible, and actual. His move toward God not only changed his life but impacted the lives of millions of people.

What is your burning bush? A devotion you read that repeated a verse that continues to show up in your life? A podcast or pastor's sermon that keeps replaying in your mind? A worship song that brought you to your knees? A stunning sunrise or sunset that almost went unnoticed?

Move toward your burning bush.

There is no failure that has gone unseen, no fear that has been ignored, no frailty that has missed His attention, and no fault that has overcome you that God has not seen. Move toward your burning bush. Allow Him to pick up the pieces of your fractured faith, reveal your potential, and show you what He can do through you. Let your potential be visual and actual, just like Moses. God may not call you to deliver a nation from bondage, but I promise what He has in store for you is no less significant to the advancement of His kingdom.

Never forget. You are a worthwhile possibility … He hasn't forgotten you.

Reflecting on What God Can Do with My Future

1. It's easy to read chapters 2 through 5 and feel hopeless, and hopeless is exactly how our enemy, Satan, wants us to feel. God has a great plan for your life that includes your fears, failures, frailties, and faults. Locate Philippians 2:13 in your Bible. Why does God work in us?

2. We often think we have to clean ourselves up and put ourselves together before God can save us. Using your Bible, turn to 1 Timothy 1:9. What is *not* the reason for Christ's saving us?

3. Why did God save us? Use John 3:16 to find your answer.

4. Since God works in us for His purpose and pleasure, and saved us because He loved us and not because of our works, this is a time for celebration. God has called you with love and purpose regardless of your "imperfections." Now what?

King David wrote beautiful words of praise after the ark of the covenant was returned to Jerusalem. The ark was the symbol of God's presence. It had been temporarily and wrongly moved from the temple, but now, it was back where it was supposed to be, where God designed it to be. Prayerfully, through the words of *Hidden Potential* and the truths of God's Word, you are where you are supposed to be, right in front of God reaching for His righteous hand (Isa. 41:10, 13) and holding tight with anticipation for the next step.

Read 1 Chronicles 16:11 from your Bible, and write David's words of instructions.

Just as God lifted the yoke of slavery from His people in Egypt, He longs to lift the yoke of slavery for us—slavery to our fears, faults, failures, and frailties. He invites us to be under the direction of His yoke, the yoke of possibility, hope, and potential, of freedom to walk out our calling in confidence, despite our fears, faults, failures, and frailties. He sees you. He sees the you that you can't yet see.

Revealing My Potential

Use the space provided to respond to the following prompt: Will you move forward? How will you move forward?

_____

_____

_____

_____

_____

Epilogue

Have you ever wondered about the design of a book cover? *How did they come up with the design? Why did they select that color? What is the significance of those elements?* I'll be honest, until I was an author, I never thought much about it. I learned quickly that covers aren't haphazardly thrown together. Each cover goes through a design process with many drafts and lots of input.

Hidden Potential is covered with magnolias in various stages of bloom. Even though I didn't choose magnolias or the color purple, I love them both. It wasn't until I prayed about how to write this final piece that I realized the place magnolias have had in my life.

As I write this epilogue, I'm at my parents' house, my childhood home, giving my mother post-surgical care. I see her fancy, special-company-coming-to-dinner dishes standing stately in the eight-foot glass mahogany china cabinet. She wanted this china so much that she made monthly payments on the twelve-place setting, complete with serving pieces, from the money she earned as a bank teller. The china pattern? Magnolias. I've always admired the beauty of these dishes … never ate off them, but always admired them.

Picture a chubby-kneed, five-year-old preschooler with fingernails chewed to the quick standing under the umbrella of the magnificent branches of a magnolia tree, the limbs weighted by the white blooms. She's waiting for her favorite friend to come outside for playtime. When her friend's class finally arrives, the two giggly girls climb the sturdy branches. After the exhausting acrobatic feat, the two sit with their backs to the world, criss-cross applesauce on the dusty ground beneath the tree to sing and slap hands in rhythm: *Mrs. Mary Mac Mac Mac all dressed in black black black with silver buttons buttons buttons up and down her back back back.* We don't climb trees or sing "Mrs. Mary Mac" anymore, but the bond formed all those years ago is as strong as the tree itself.

Then in 1996, Scott and I built our first home … and lived to tell about it. (If you have ever custom built a home, you know what I am talking about.) I could not wait to decorate our new home on Kullana Lane. Like many women, the kitchen was my first priority. The right tile, countertops, wood floors, appliances, cabinets, and of course, the decor. Without hesitation, I selected magnolias. Canister set, placemats, and serving pieces all boasted the white budding flower.

Until the writing and research for this final punctuation mark, I only knew of the magnolia's beauty. As in all of God's creation, beauty is just part of the story. There are many spiritual parallels from which we can draw encouragement. Our Creator is a masterful designer. Every single thing He creates has purpose and potential.

The bloom of the magnolia is delicate in appearance; however, the tree is very hardy and resilient against harsh conditions. It can adapt to and survive in a variety of climates and other environmental challenges. Perhaps this is why the flower represents endurance, eternity, and long life. Femininity and purity are represented in the tender soft flower as well.

A woman walking in tandem with her Creator is a force to be reckoned with. Whether she stands five-foot tall and needs a stool to reach the top shelf in her kitchen or she's six-foot-three and with a running start from half court can dunk a basketball, a woman and her God make a powerful team. Delicate and soft to the touch, yet spiritually strong enough to move a mountain with her prayers.

Just like the beautiful skin tones of God's final and splendid creation, man and woman, magnolia flowers are available in a variety of colors. The diverse magnolias can stand side by side and complement any garden. *Red and yellow, black and white,* we are all precious in His sight. There's no need to compete; we can complete each other in the beauty with which God has adorned us.

Some magnolia trees, like the grandiflora, or southern magnolia, can grow eighty feet tall with a diameter of thirty-six inches. One would assume that a tree of this magnitude would need a deep root system to sustain it. The magnolia, however, survives and thrives with rope-like roots that reach horizontally rather than vertically. As women following God, we survive and thrive in relationship together, spreading and reaching out to one another. Together, roping each other arm in arm, we stand strong to weather the storms of life.

Whether representing Louisiana as the state flower or becoming the central theme of a blockbuster Hollywood movie (1989's *Steel*

Magnolias), these blooms symbolize beauty, strength, and purity. This, however, is how they appear *after* the stages of bloom. There's a process. Each bloom has potential, but it must receive the right care and nutrients in order to reach its full potential.

At first, the cone-shaped flower is brown tinged and has what appears to be a prickly growth on its fuzzy exterior. Then the cone turns pink with red seeds growing and turning outward. In bloom, it bursts at the seams. The white petals slowly reach out as if to tell the world and shout in worship, *I'm beautiful. My Creator saw my potential all along.*

Stay close to your Creator (God) and get the right nourishment (His Word), my friends. One day soon you will stretch your arms open wide in worship and say, *"I'm a beautiful woman of God, full of potential, and my Creator knew it all the time."*

Notes

Chapter 1: What God Can Do

1. StudyLight.org, s.v. "*apistía*," accessed October 19, 2019, www.studylight.org /lexicons/greek/570.html.

2. "Feeble Faith Appealing to a Strong Savior," Charles Spurgeon Sermon Collection, accessed October 19, 2019, http://thekingdomcollective.com /spurgeon/sermon/2881/.

3. Bible Hub, s.v. "*ginóskō*," accessed October 20, 2019, https://biblehub.com /greek/1097.htm.

4. "How Does God's Sovereignty Work Together with Free Will?," GotQuestions.org, July 26, 2019, www.gotquestions.org/free-will-sovereign.html.

5. Bible Hub, s.v. "*eidó*," accessed October 20, 2019, https:// biblehub.com/greek/1492.htm.

Chapter 2: What God Can Do through My Failures

1. J. Hampton Keathley III, "Mark #17: The Wisdom to Deal with Failure," Bible.org, May 26, 2004, https://bible.org/seriespage/mark-17-wisdom -deal-failure#P2343_659843.

2. Bible Hub, s.v. "*nikaó*," accessed October 20, 2019, https://biblehub.com/greek/3528.htm.

Chapter 3: What God Can Do through My Fears

1. "Fear Factor," Wikipedia, accessed October 20, 2019, https://en.wikipedia.org/wiki/Fear_Factor.

2. Bible Hub, s.v. "*menó*," accessed October 20, 2019, https://biblehub.com/greek/3306.htm.

3. R. C. Sproul, *Now, That's a Good Question!: Answers to More Than 300 Frequently Asked Questions about Life and Faith* (Carol Stream, IL: Tyndale, 1996), quoted at "Throughout the Bible We Are Told to Fear God. What Does That Mean?," Ligonier Ministries, accessed October 21, 2019, www.ligonier.org/learn/qas/throughout-bible-we-are-told-fear-god-what-does-me/.

4. "What Is a Theophany? What Is a Christophany?," GotQuestions.org, July 26, 2019, www.gotquestions.org/theophany-Christophany.html.

5. Max Lucado, *Make Every Day Count* (Nashville: Thomas Nelson, 2012), 88.

Chapter 4: What God Can Do through My Frailties

1. "Joni Eareckson Tada Shares Her Story," YouTube, posted by Joni and Friends, January 28, 2014, www.youtube.com/watch?v=VVXJ8GyLgt0.

2. "Joni Eareckson Tada," www.youtube.com/watch?v=VVXJ8GyLgt0.

3. Louie Giglio, *I Am Not but I Know I AM: Welcome to the Story of God* (Colorado Springs: Multnomah, 2012), 33, 35.

4. Joni Eareckson Tada, *Hope … the Best of Things* (Wheaton, IL: Crossway Books, 2008), 29.

5. Henry Blackaby, quoted in Ken Blanchard and Phil Hodges, *Lead Like Jesus: Lessons for Everyone from the Greatest Leadership Role Model of All Time* (Nashville: Thomas Nelson, 2005), 199.

6. Bible Hub, s.v. "*kauchaomai*," accessed October 21, 2019, https://biblehub.com/greek/2744.htm.

Chapter 5: What God Can Do through My Faults

1. Matthew Henry, "Exodus 4," in *Concise Commentary on the Whole Bible* (originally published 1701–1721), available at Bible Hub, accessed October 21, 2019, https://biblehub.com/commentaries/mhc/exodus/4.htm.

About the Author

Wendy is the wife of Scott, mother of Blaire and Griffin, author, speaker, and Bible study teacher. She loves lazy Sundays watching golf with her husband, thrift-store shopping with her daughter, and watching building shows with her son.

Wendy is the author of *Wait and See: Finding Peace in God's Pauses and Plans* and the *Wait and See Participant's Guide: A Six-Session Study on Waiting Well*, as well as the *Yes, No, and Maybe: Living with the God of Immeasurably More* book, study guide, and video series. She is a contributing author to the *Real-Life Women's Devotional Bible*, *Encouragement for Today: Devotions for Daily Living*, *The Reason We Speak*, and *God's Purpose for Every Woman*.

She leads women all over the world to life change through her in-depth online Bible studies. Down-to-earth and transparent, Wendy teaches in a way that women feel she is speaking directly to their hearts. She has led thousands of women through her Read Thru the Word (RTW) study of the *One Year Chronological Bible*. To grow your faith and passion for God's Word, see information about Wendy's RTW class at wendypope.org/online-studies.

Her messages are filled with biblical insights but sprinkled with just the right amount of humor to help her audiences see she is a real, everyday woman. Wendy inspires her audiences to:

- make spending time in God's Word each day a priority
- look for God working around them every day
- view life with a God-first perspective

To bring the message of *Hidden Potential* or another of Wendy's inspiring topics to your next event, contact speakercoordinator@proverbs31.org.

Connect with Wendy

Website: wendypope.org
Email: wendy@wendypope.org
Facebook: www.facebook.com/WendyPopeOfficial
Twitter: @wendybpope
Instagram: Wendy_Pope
Pinterest: www.pinterest.com/wendypope67

Proverbs 31
MINISTRIES

ABOUT PROVERBS 31 MINISTRIES

If you were inspired by *Hidden Potential* and desire to deepen your own personal relationship with Jesus Christ, I encourage you to connect with Proverbs 31 Ministries.

Proverbs 31 Ministries exists to be a trusted friend who will take you by the hand and walk by your side, leading you one step closer to the heart of God through:

- Free online daily devotions
- First 5 Bible study app
- Online Bible Studies
- Podcast
- COMPEL Writer Training
- She Speaks Conference
- Books and resources

For more information about Proverbs 31 Ministries, visit: www.Proverbs31.org.

Bible Credits

Unless otherwise noted, all Scripture quotations are taken from THE HOLY BIBLE, NEW INTERNATIONAL VERSION®, NIV® Copyright © 1973, 1978, 1984, 2011 by Biblica, Inc.® Used by permission. All rights reserved worldwide.

Scripture quotations marked AMP are taken from the Amplified® Bible, copyright © 2015 by The Lockman Foundation. Used by permission. (www.Lockman.org).

Scripture quotations marked AMPC are taken from the Amplified® Bible Classic, copyright © 1954, 1987 by The Lockman Foundation. Used by permission. (www.Lockman.org).

Scripture quotations marked CEV are taken from the Contemporary English Version © 1991, 1995 by American Bible Society. Used by permission.

Scripture quotations marked CJB are taken from the Complete Jewish Bible. Copyright © 1998 David H. Stern. All rights reserved.

Scripture quotations marked ERV are taken from the Easy-to-Read Version. Copyright © 2006 by Bible League International.